Touches of Life
in
Time and Space

Barbara Knickerbocker

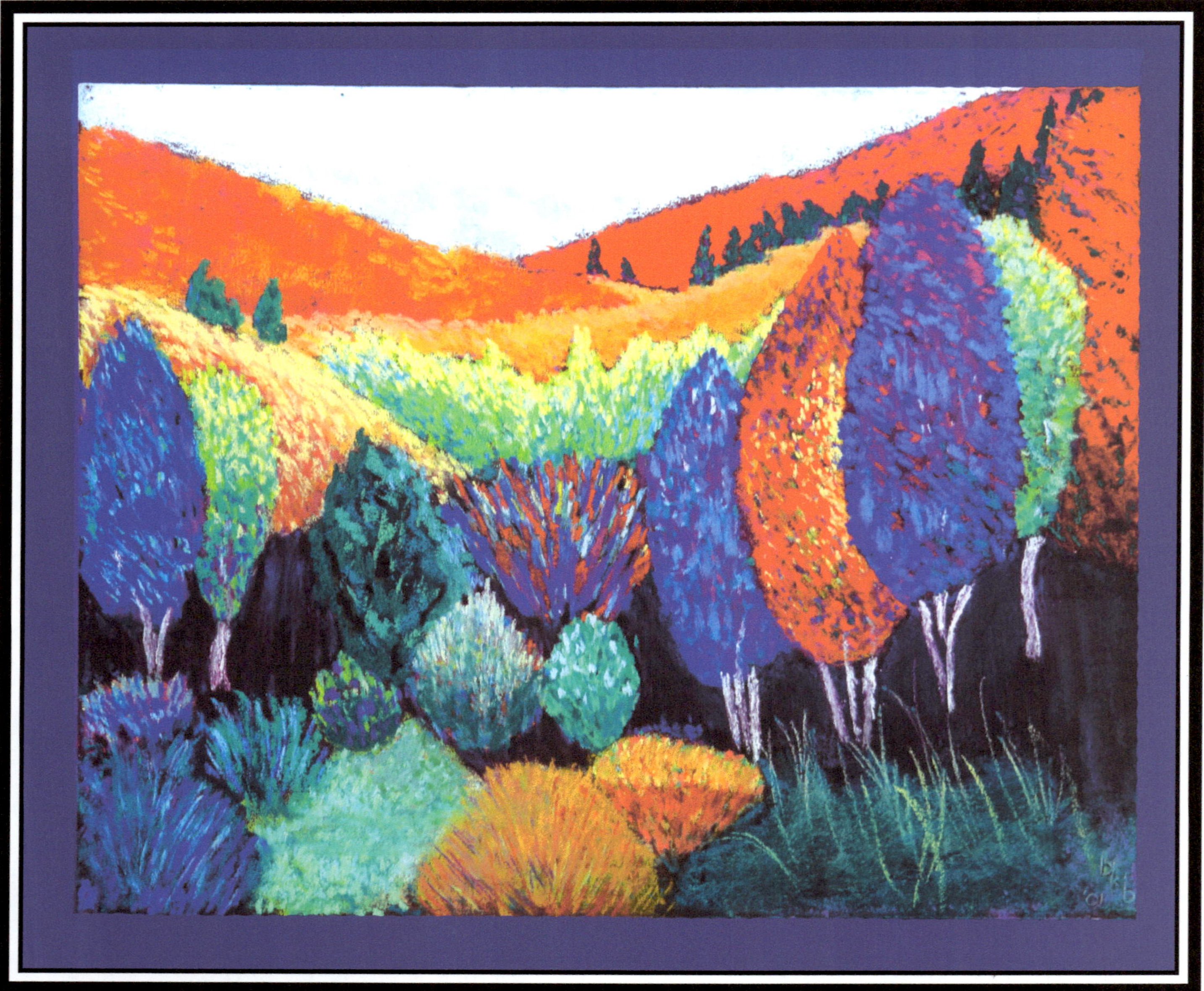

Vertical Foliage

Touches of Life
in
Time and Space

Barbara Knickerbocker

BKB Press
New London, New Hampshire

Touches of Life in Time and Space

Barbara Knickerbocker

Published by BKB Press, New London, New Hampshire

Book design and typesetting by RSBPress, Waitsfield, Vermont
Photography by Alan Nyire and Kitty Werner

For further information about the art, contact BKB Press.

Footnotes within the poetry are located in the Addenda on page 92.

The poems *Naptime of a Three-Year-Old; F O U R; Smiley; My Mind, My Reservoir* were first published in *Clustered Together, Poems from the Pavilion,* The Gateway Press Inc., Baltimore, MD, 1996. Reprinted with adaptations and with permission.

BKB Press
103 Hilltop Place
New London, New Hampshire 03257

ISBN 978-09817768-2-8

Cover painting: Earthquake in Egypt

Acknowledgments

My appreciation is extended to the following:

Kristopher Calnan, MFA and Cheryl Lewis Wolf, MFA, both of the Sharon Art Center, Sharon, New Hampshire for their instruction, mentoring, and guidance to enrich the innate feelings I had for abstract art. Kristopher Calnan, MFA for introducing me to the art of the Russian Avant-garde.

Jeanne Carbonetti, artist and author of Chester, Vermont for her inspiration, support, and instruction in watercolor.

The instructors at the Bennington College four-week Seminars and Workshops at Bennington, Vermont 1992–1994 to include, the late Liam Rector, Director and renown poet, Percival Everett, Ph.D., Professor of English, University of Southern California, and Elinor Lipman with whom I also studied at the Simmons College Writers Program.

The instructors in writing and poetry workshops and classes at the Omega Institute, Rhinebeck, New York between 1996 and 1998: Gabrielle Rico, Ph.D., William Least-Heat Moon, and Andrei Codrescu.

Anne Mausolff for her dedicated interest, time and contributions in reviewing the contents.

Kay Wear Draper, former Professor of Linguistics and Oral Communication, Worcester Polytechnical Institute, Worcester, Massachusetts, Millard Hunter, history scholar, Ruth Reed, and Susan MacFarlane and other friends who have graciously shared their comments and suggestions.

Alan Nyire and Kitty Werner for the photography.

Sue Publicover for her editing assistance.

Kitty Werner, RSBPress, graphic designer for developing the print and photographic units with artistic skill.

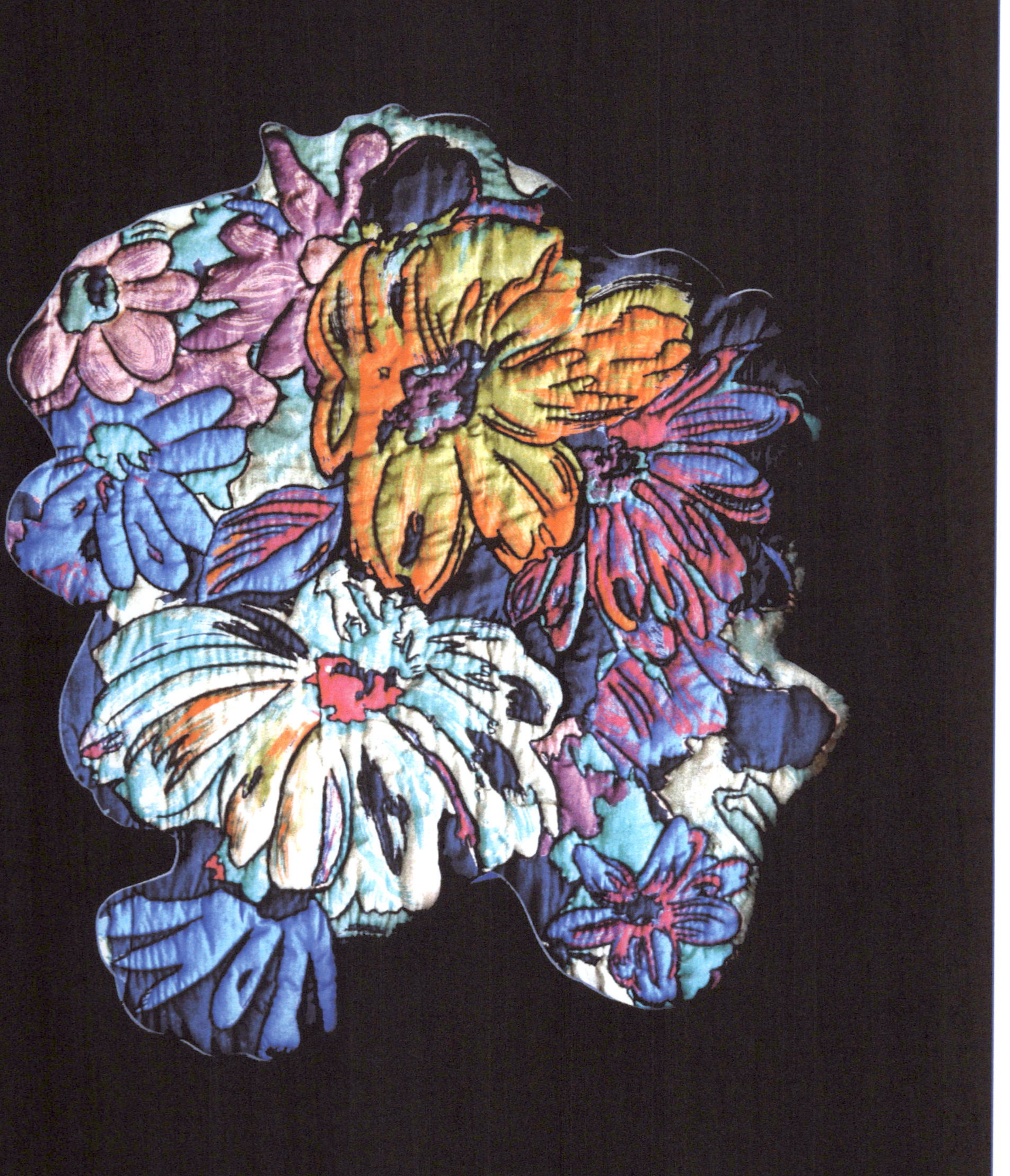

Original Piece of Embroidered Art 1989

To my mother

who

always had a good sense of humor
and could laugh at herself

but to hear her try to repeat
a joke she had heard

was as funny as the joke itself
often skipping to the punch line first.

Never did she skip a stitch in sewing
and I am ever so indebted to her

for all the thread and needle skills
she shared with such diligence and joy.

— March 26, 2006

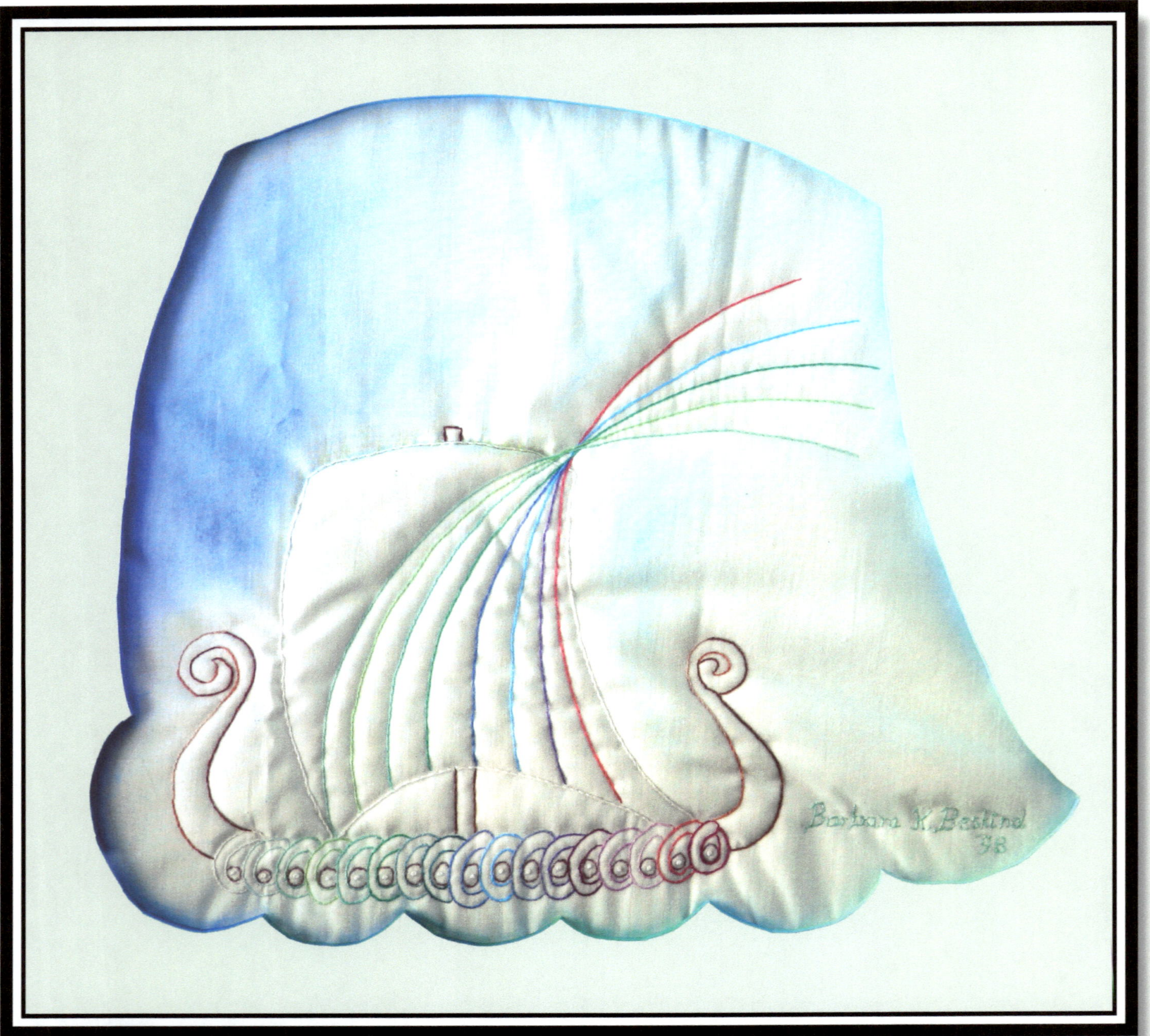

Viking Ship

Introduction

Touches of Life in Time and Space comprises a collection of 40 pieces of poetry and more than 50 works of art. These poems range from history that impacts ancestral and family stories to personal life-experience, told with humor and satire. This book is the second in a series of "windows on history." The first in this series is *Powder Keg,*[1] written both as an autobiography and as a documentation of history that surrounded my early ancestors in Europe and in pre-colonial America. The third "window on history" is scheduled for release in 2009, and will be entitled *Touches of Art and the Impact of the Russian Avant-garde.*

Rarely can one trace family origins back 25 generations as my father's side, the Knickerbocker/Knickerbakker/van Wye family claims. Our branch of the Knickerbocker family stems from Laurence, second son of the family founder in this country, Harmon Jansen Knickerbakker who arrived from Holland in 1674. This is depicted in *Powder Keg.*

As a child, I was well aware of how much my parents had hoped for a male heir to carry the family name, bloodline, and history. However, their first child, Donald, died at birth, and I bore no children. Thus I felt a compelling personal need to preserve traces of family history.

I discovered a cohesive web of historical events in Europe in the 16th and 17th centuries and in pre-colonial America. I present this in Part I of *Touches of Life in Time and Space* through the historical "scaffolding" of ancestors on each side of the family.

One ancestor on my mother's side, a Walloon from the part of The Netherlands then called the Belgic Lands, arrived in Nieuw Amsterdam[2] in 1634. Another, a Huguenot fugitive who fled La Tremblade prison in 1687, first settled in New Orford, near Boston. Yet another, from the Palatines of Germany, arrived in 1710. Five or six were passengers on the *Mayflower.*

Other forbears in this family provide a colorful, often humorous, backdrop to these narrative poems. While presented as individual entities, these poems are often more enjoyable when viewed as part of an integrated whole within Part I.

Poems in Parts II through V are linked by a visible thread of continuity. They characterize various stages in the life experience of my family and me. *Touches of Life in Time and Space* uniquely integrates my abiding interest in history, writing, and art.

My interest in art does not focus on developing expertise in watercolors or pastels, but rather on a fast-paced, innovative mode of exploration throughout a range of artistic forms.

My interest in history arises primarily out of the group of people called the Walloons[3] who figure in my mother's distant ancestry. Long before the Protestant Reformation, the Belgic Walloons were recognized throughout Europe for their advanced technological skills, inventive spirit, and innovative problem-solving abilities.

My curiosity is aroused by the remote possibility that some genetic predisposition has contributed to a relentless creative drive of my own, throughout diverse endeavors.[4]

Whenever I have engaged in creative problem-solving in my professional career, my writing, my artistic exploration, or in my everyday life, I am imbued with a joyful, energizing, fulfilling elixir of life. This creative passion is embodied in *Touches of Life in Time and Space* by melding history with poetry and art.

The question lingers: could the spirit of innovation of those distant Walloon ancestors have been sufficiently preserved in the genes, to make its imprint on me? It feels that way.

In recent years, I have become fascinated by the innovative exploration of the art of the Russian avant-garde that occurred between 1910 and 1922.[5] I am profoundly aware that the innovative exploration they strongly embraced is inherently akin to my own. Thus another piece of life's mysterious puzzle fits into place, as depicted in the poems of Part V.

1 *Powder Keg,* by Barbara Knickerbocker, was published by BKB Press, New London, New Hampshire, 2008.

2 original Dutch and Walloon spelling

3 Walloons were those people who lived below the River Waal, an arm of the Rhine delta that flows to the North Sea. These early Walloons of the Belgic tribes were reputed to have been the most tenacious, fierce fighters that Caesar's legions ever encountered. See Addendum A for details.

4 Creative problem-solving constituted a major element of my long professional career as an occupational therapist who specialized in the treatment and rehabilitation of physically-impaired and learning-disordered children and adults. For this, I designed and patented pieces of equipment to foster the patient's improvement.

5 My passion for abstract art was initially sparked by a love of the lines and forms in geometry, but was kindled anew by studying the history and work of the Russian avant-garde artists, expressed through poems of Part IV.

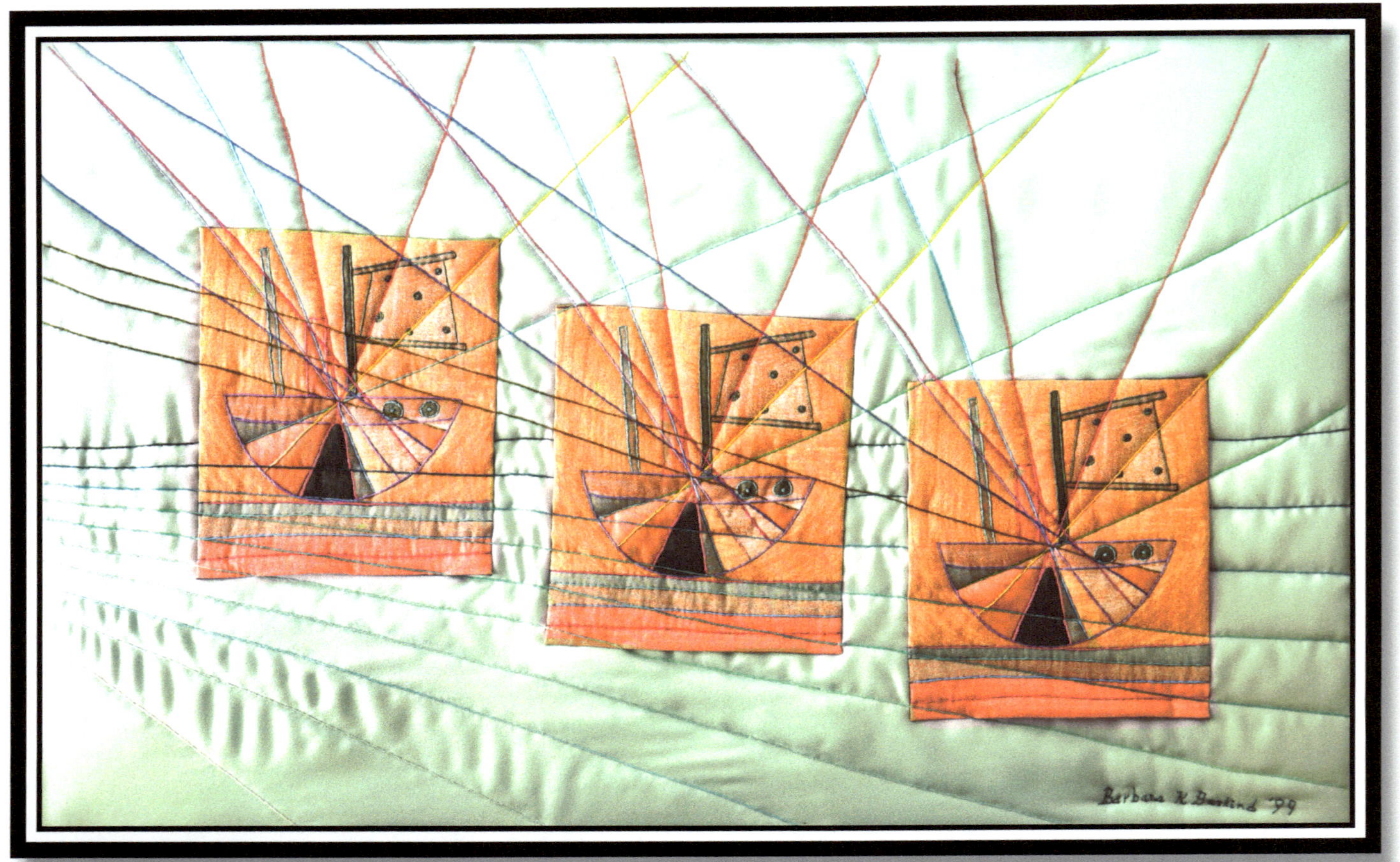

The *Nina*, the *Pinta*, and the *Santa Maria*

Preface

Some of this poetry was written in 1995 and 1996 when I attended various poetry and writing courses at the Omega Institute in Rhinebeck, New York. The town of Rhinebeck is located only 20 miles from where I grew up, in Bangall, New York. Early history of Rhinebeck figures in the poetry of Part I.

The poems "Flax to Freedom" written in 1995 and "Letter to Grandma 'K.'" written in 2003 are included in my book, *Powder Keg*. Inspiration for the main body of poetry in *Touches of Life in Time and Space* followed in 2006.

Early seeds of my interest in sculptured art originated in a ceramic course at Syracuse University in 1945. (See *Bear*, page 72.) This informed the expression of bas-relief hand-embroidery and sculpture-cut mats in my current phase of artistic development that began in 1997. It was then that I started the study of abstract art at the Sharon Art Center in Sharon, New Hampshire. All the art pictured here has been produced since 1997 except for the afore-mentioned sculptured bear, the 1989 original piece of bas-relief hand-embroidery, (see page 6) and a simple pastel (see page 78) .

In 1998 and 1999, I took private instruction in watercolors from Jeanne Carbonetti of Chester, Vermont. It was Jeanne who nurtured the innovative combination of embroidery with my art.

My love of hand-stitching led me to develop what I call "thread and needle" art. First, I embellished printed fabrics with embroidery for wall hangings. (See *Vermont History in the Abstract*, page 68.) Later, I embroidered my own watercolor and pastel art, some of which was done directly on cotton or silk. (See *Life's Many Stages and Interactions*, page 90.) Other watercolors were transposed from paper onto Egyptian cotton for embroidery. (See *Wild Orchid*, page 82.) By placing soft padding between a top and bottom layer of fabric, I produced a "bas-relief" effect.[1]

Original sculpture-cut mats surround many of these pieces of embroidered art. I attach a layer of mat board to $^{3}/_{16}$" foam core. Then I cut out the interior with a scroll saw. The contoured inner edge is often shaded with pastels. (See *Viking Ship*, page 8.)

"Cut-apart" art, an original technique, is achieved by placing a sheet of white paper over a black one, and after drawing the "abstract" I cut the two at the same time. Then I rotate and interpose the pieces to create interesting new abstract forms. (See *End of the River*, page 18.)

In another aspect of my artistic exploration, I apply pastels with the tip of my finger to two layers of tracing paper, thus creating greater depth of shading. (See *Churches of the Kremlin*, page 76.}

The area of my deepest interest has been to investigate the early evolution of abstract art by the Russian avant-garde (1910 –1922). This has inspired me to make several trips to Russia to study this art and learn about the artists. (See *My rendition of Popova's* Painterly Architectonics, 1918, page 68.)

I have enjoyed teaching the History of the Russian Avant-garde Art at the Adventures in Learning Program, a non-credit course for senior citizens at the Colby–Sawyer College in New London, New Hampshire.

1 This means an impression of low, surface sculpture.

Table of Contents

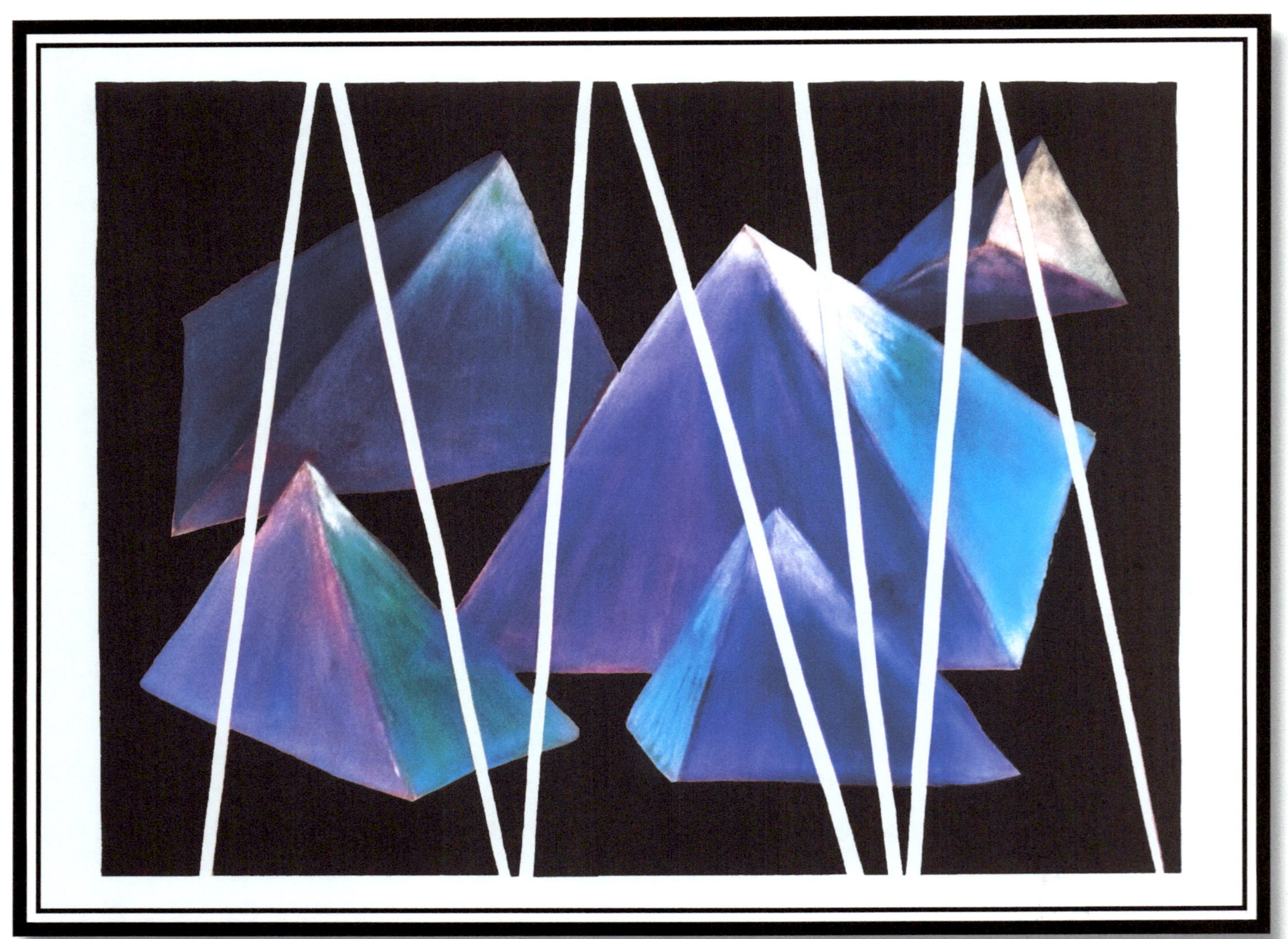

Pyramids in Abstract

Poems

Part I

I want to trace the fingerprint,
    I want to trace those rings,
        those family imprints
            on the face of history.

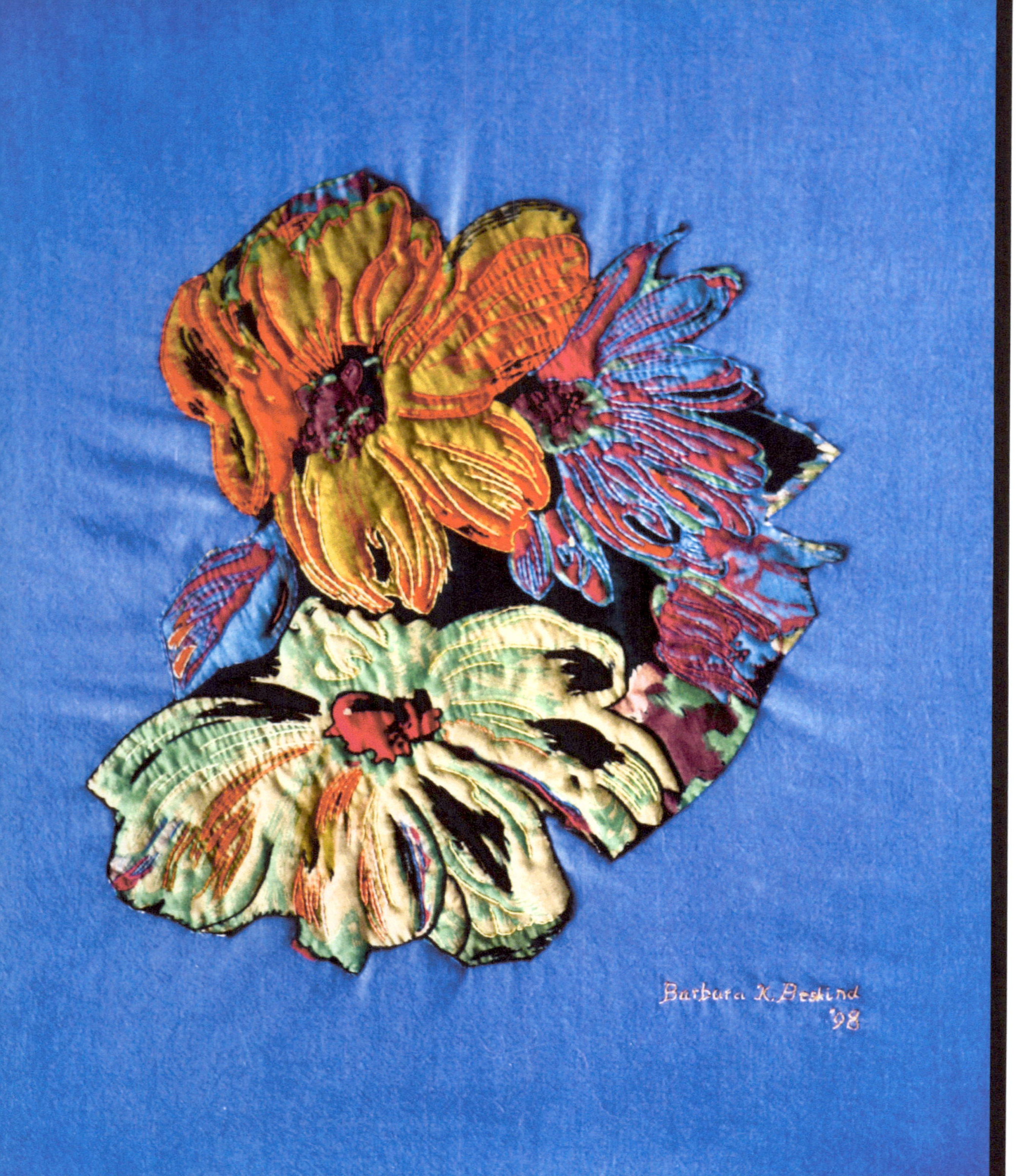

Dahlias

A Fingerprint of Mankind

A fingerprint of mankind through the ages,
my family's ages—a fingerprint that links us all.

I want to trace those rings,
those family imprints on the face of history.

My father was an investigator in the FBI
but I am the investigator now.

I investigate my family's early origins,
livelihoods, loyalties, and beliefs.

I inherit his investigative nature
to research relevant rhythms

from patterned rings, to the depths
of generations before,

from Bangall to Albany,
to the Dutch in North Brabant

to the Walloon provinces
in the Belgic Lands.

I want to trace those rings,
those family imprints of history,
of history revisited and revised.

No two fingerprints the same,
no two faces alike.

This is the imprint
on one person—ME.
I am the investigator now.

1996

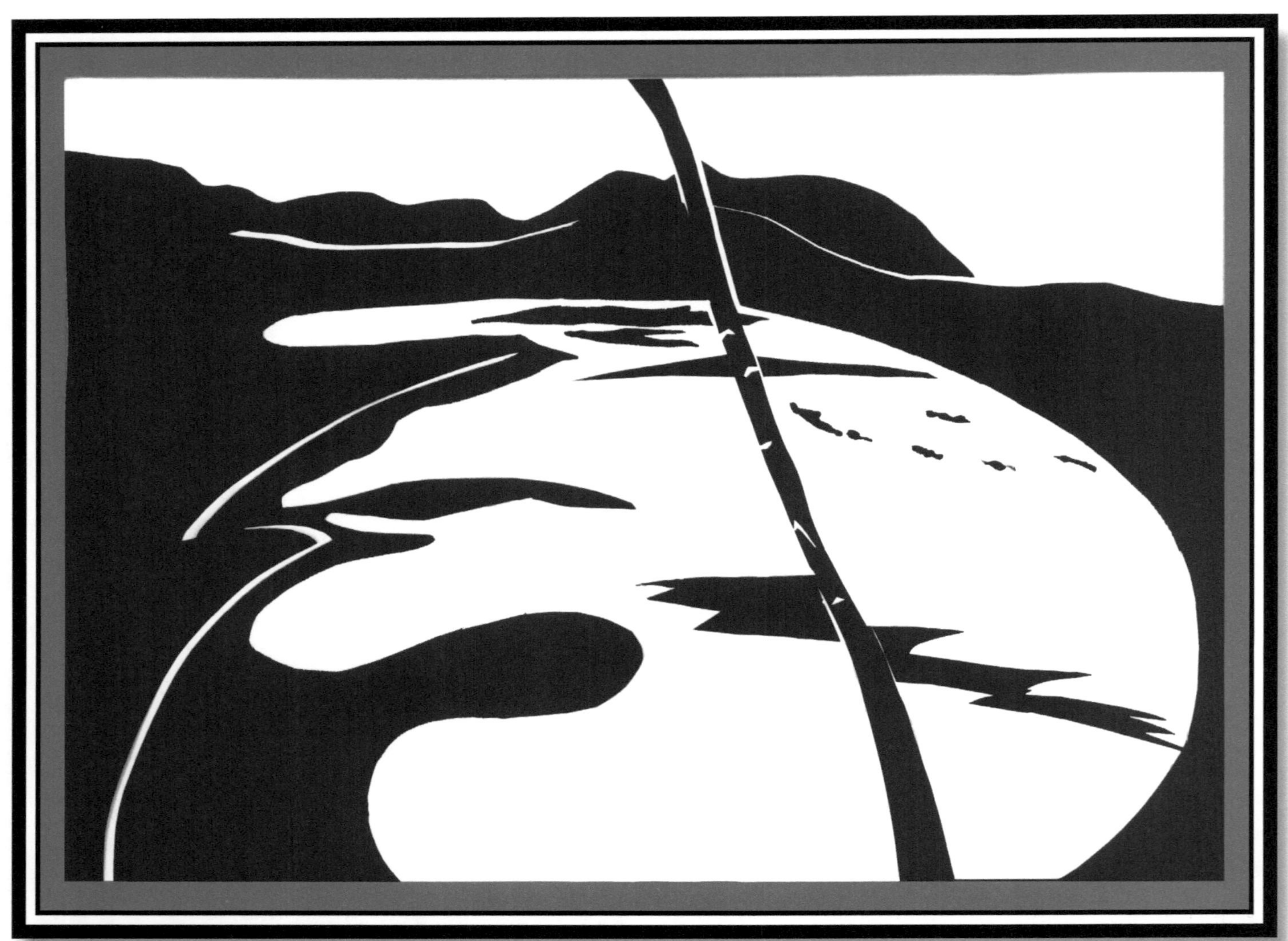

End of the River

Surprise Aboard Hudson's *Half Moon*

Here is another story of Henry Hudson and his crew,
a twist about his voyage to the New World heard by few.

This may be speculation, but there's evidence
of quite a different story than that now given credence.

Henry could have been the "wrong-way Corrigan"[1] of his time,
since he was to sail north, on the third voyage in his prime.[2]

Hudson finished his cup
of strong breakfast tea,
to stroll along the Thames, past masts
ready for the sea.
He clenched two sets of
parchment under his arm.
Their contents, if known,
would have caused alarm.

One roll was loosely wound
and slightly askew,
the other firm and round
was sealed from view.
For a year, he had studied
the maps, entranced.
Tales he heard on the docks
may have been well enhanced.

These stories claimed that
wide estuaries galore
indented a distant coastline
he intended to explore.
It was mainly the account
of Captain William Smith,
contemporary and trusted friend,
that confirmed his plans to shift

the route he was embarking on
for the next ocean adventure,
but he needed to proceed without
incurring corporate censure.
A few blocks from the docks,
Merchant Adventurers[3] cast fear
on brave navigators who
charted the waters far from a pier.

Hudson's grandfather was a founder,
his father, a member
of this London holding company that had
condemned him in September,
for twice failing to push
through thick Arctic ice
for a better route to the Orient
to buy tea, silk, and spice.

Thus, when Henry approached
the Merchants to request
funds for his next voyage, to a man,
they were unimpressed.
Then, he took his petition
to a Dutch Embassy official,
or was invited to consider
a voyage mutually beneficial.

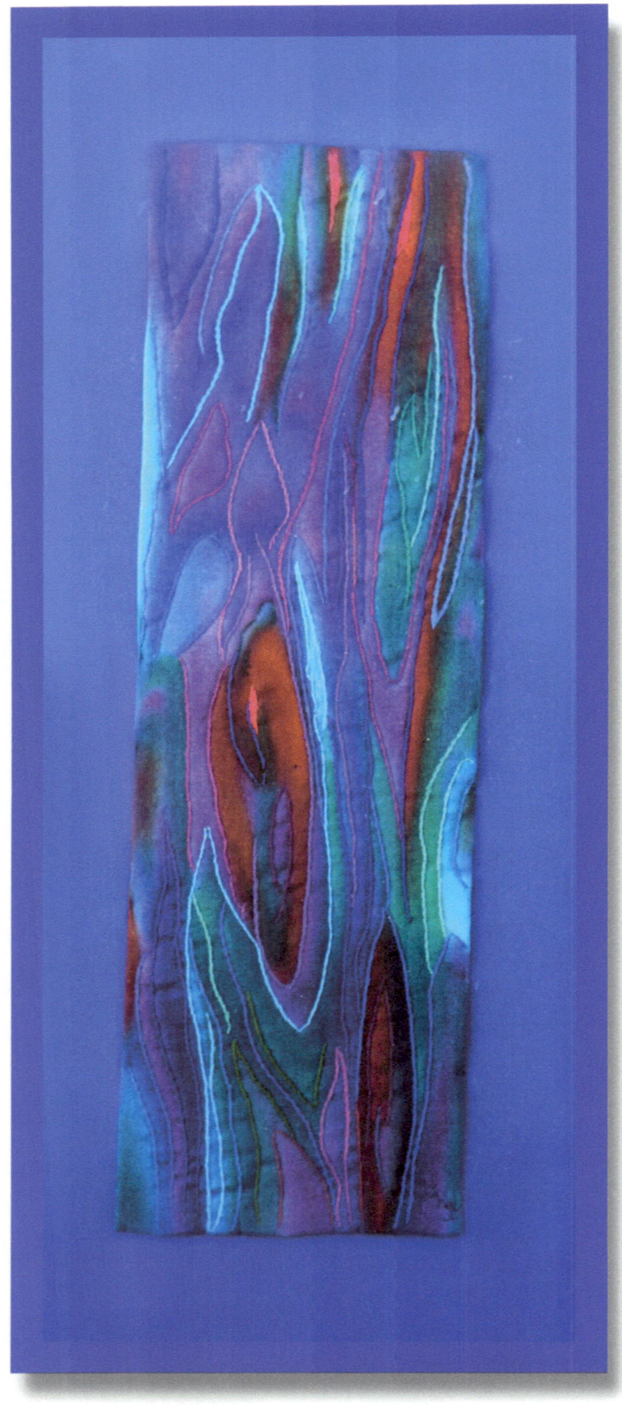

Northern Lights

Hudson kept his secret secure,
giving no one access
to plans he felt this time
would assure him success.
He was to follow the route
they clearly prescribed
to map claims for the Dutch State
their East India Company defined.

He was to find a northern route
by the Barents Sea
along Siberia's coast
with Nova Zemyla on the lee.
Dutch officials decided five months
of sunshine would be
sufficient to warm Arctic waters
and open uncharted seas.

For years the Dutch had feared
this seasoned explorer
would sail again for the
English and then discover
that ice-locked passage
nature had banned,
the route they needed to unlock,
exploit, and then expand.

Desperate from losing too many
ships, goods, and mates,[4]
they called him to Amsterdam
to discuss sailing dates.
As Captain, he chose the men:
half were Englishmen he knew
plus Dutch East India Company sailors,
a sun-tanned, salty crew.

Along the Norwegian coast
past Stavanger, Bergen, Trondheim,[5]
he headed toward Hammerfest,
above the Arctic Circle and then,

ice flows thickened. The warm-water
    sailors Hudson had chosen
reacted just as he expected
    when the sea became frozen.

With less incentive than he
    to fulfill their alleged goal,
despite mittens, caps and coats,
    they refused to leave the hold.
In unison, they insisted
    they wouldn't climb the rigging.
Hudson foiled their anger
    and called them to a briefing.

Striving hard to hide
    his smile from the rest,
he ordered his men to: "Sail,
    sail into the sunset, sail to the west."
Surprised, but relieved, they turned
    their frosted beards to follow
their Captain's command to sail
    toward waters warm and shallow.

Angers melted like icebergs
    as oceans became warmer.
Now the crew willingly supported
    their hardy globe-plotter.
Finally they spotted land and sailed
    within sight of shore.
From Newfoundland to the Chesapeake,
    they searched each tidal bore.

Now, Hudson unrolled his long-sealed maps
    drawn from deep study and old sea lore.
These held promise for the trade route
    he was zealous to explore.
A broad, sheltered harbor sparked new hope
    for the prize that they sought,
so the Dutch could sail to China, and return
    with goods that they'd bought.

Hudson searched far upriver,
    past sparkling creek-runs,
and sent out men in a dingy,
    northern fathoms to plumb.
He hoped for deep rivers
    feeding in from the west
so he could sail farther
    and resolve this quest.

North of the Mohawk
    on the west bank of land
sailors came ashore and found
    muscular natives, deeply tanned.
Land-starved at home, the Dutch
    envisioned returning soon
to this rich landscape
    they named Half Moon.

This had nothing to do
    with the name of their ship,
but for the crescent-shaped hills
    as the late sun dipped.
When the crew returned
    steep falls were reported.[6]
Hudson sensed his life-long goal
    again had been thwarted.

Henry couldn't foresee this river
    would carry his name,
impact world commerce
    and rightly claim art fame.
This is my tale about the third
    voyage of Hudson and crew.
If true, his discovery, by chance or by ruse,
    merits a fresh historical review.

2006

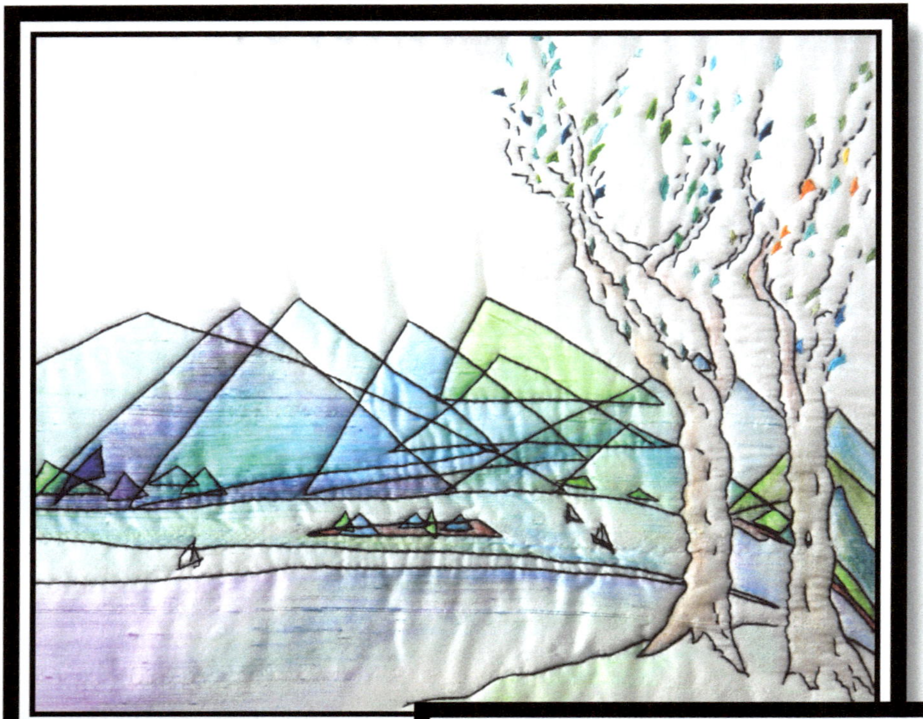

Adirondacks in the Abstract

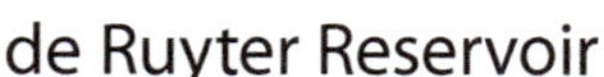

de Ruyter Reservoir

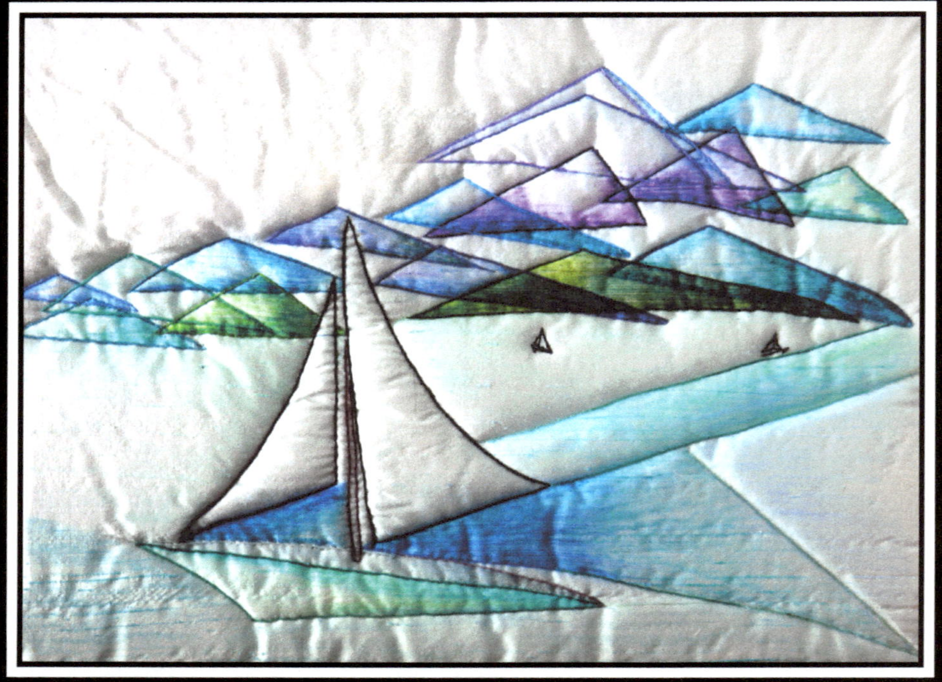

The Other Half Moon[1]

Hudson's crew found rich promise
in the land they named "Half Moon,"
but failed to meet their pledge
to return and settle soon.

From a personal point of view
I consider their dream was realized.
Their goal became an opportunity
another Dutchman recognized.

As a child born in Bommel
Harmon Jansen van Wye[2]
heard great stories
of a fertile place far, far away.

This stretch of land
beyond the ocean's navigation,
at the end of a mighty river,
challenged his youthful imagination.

Wounded in the Battle of Solebay
under Admiral de Ruyter's command,
Harmon could no longer return to Bommel,
to his family, home, or land.[3]

Childhood stories flooded his mind
as he sailed in June[4] from Amsterdam
to search the west bank of the Hudson River
where that promised spot, "Half Moon" would stand.[5]

In the light of a full moon,
Harmon came there to stay
and began his family of seven,
their name no longer van Wye.

Harmon Jansen Knickerbocker, from whom
all Knickerbockers are descended,
adopted this country, and
aggressively kept it defended.

Thus a countryman from Bommel,
unknown to any of Hudson's crew,
fulfilled their unlikely dream,
sixty-five years beyond their view.[6]

2006

A Reluctant Pilgrim

In order to keep their faith secure
Separatists left old England's shore,
for Holland's city of Leyden.
Twelve years later, as Puritans
they moved again
to preserve their religious purity.

The Merchant Adventurers
helped to finance
the *Mayflower's* voyage
that brought hopeful Puritans
for freedom of religion
to a new and productive land.

They were brought ashore
at the unplanned destination
of breezy Cape Cod
instead of the Virginia Colony
where crops could thrive
in those warmer climes.

Many Puritans were indebted
to their backers for passage.
Richard Warren was sent over
as bursar to assure
the Merchant Adventurers
were paid in full measure.

Being from London, and not
the Leyden community,
Richard never expected to stay
past guaranteeing that
through crop yields,
the Puritan's debts were fully repaid.

Therefore, it was under duress
he signed the *Mayflower Compact*—
the first written decree
of law and order
in this wild, this virgin,
and vast new country.

Circumstances soon forced him,
like Myles Standish, to stay,
to become part
of the Plymouth Colony
among the Pilgrims
we know about today.

Richard's son married Mehitable.
Descendants became Sissons,
originators of the line that became mine,
on my Grandmother Ham's mother's side.
Near Poughkeepsie, members
of this family, named Titus, still reside.

Among those who comprised the Plymouth Colony
traceable in our forest of family trees
were ersatz Pilgrims Myles Standish,
Francis Cooke, and his family who
were less colorful to me than the originator
of the Warrens, the Sissons, and Wing families.

It was not the Puritans, you see,
but a virtually unknown group
of ancestral residents,
the courageous, spirited,
displaced Belgic Walloons
who fascinated me.

They arrived in Nieuw Amsterdam
on the *Brindled Cow.*
It was the name of this ship
and is passengers
who intrigued me most,
and I wanted to know how—

Walloon Reformists on my mother's side
fled the tyranny
of Spanish oppression to hide,
north of Lille, in the town of Kortyk
near the flaxfields
of Tournai.

2006

Those *Mayflower* Passengers

From a 21st century point of view,
counting only the parents and their parents
back twenty generations in review,
one person's ancestors
four hundred years before,
exceeds in number one million,
eighty-four thousand and more.

Conversely, calculated on the possibility
a new child-bearing generation
began within a twenty-year duration,
if each had but two children, their descendants
would equal the same number, in essence.
However, not two children, but ten
or more, were nearer the norm back then.

These calculations would then project
ten million passengers or more,
had arrived inadvertently
on our snow-blown shore.

Thus the claims of all those Americans,
who list as ancestors, some pious and dour,
passengers on that illustrious founding ship,
the leaky, creaky, old *Mayflower.*

Most *Mayflower* descendants,
it is assumed, claim to convey
that in the year 1620, their
ancestor arrived the same day.

Research finds, however
the *Mayflower* made eleven trips more
to transport hundreds of other
passengers to these pristine shores.

These two factors alone help to account
for the millions and millions of ancestors,
who allegedly crowded the British dock
for that celebrated voyage to Plymouth Rock.

2006

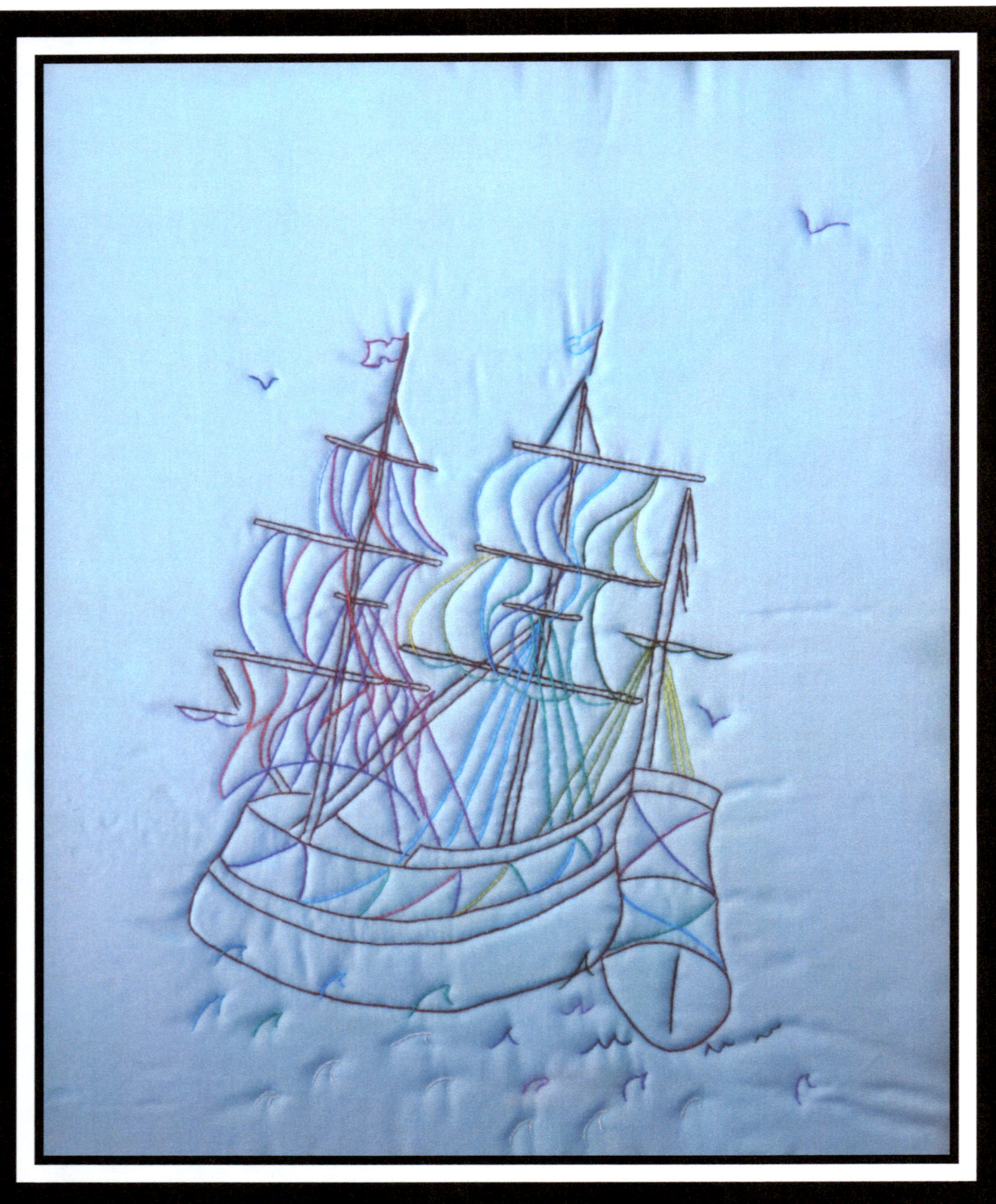

The *Mayflower*

The Miles Standish Cocktail Party[1]

When the engraved invitation arrived
my father winced, and groaned inside.
Predictably, he dreaded an event this dire,
bound to be a grandiose family "high-wire."

Stiff double envelopes encased a request.
Its center-spaced statement invited guests,
not as though they were coming for fun,
but as if sentenced for a misdeed they'd done.

Generations after the *Mayflower* landed,
another Miles Standish was newly commanded
to sit in the legislature as a state law-giver.
His home rose high above the Hudson River.[2]

Distantly related on my mother's side,
we were not in their social strata, nor economic tide.
With my father unemployed, our country existence
mainly depended on a gardening subsistence.

As the Great Depression ended, the most hearty,
stylish event was the late-afternoon "Cocktail Party."
This was foreign to our family who never imbibed.
No one we knew entertained, they just tried to survive.

Unprecedented then, was a couple's divorce.
In our family not only was it rare, it was worse!
That wife, "that" Mrs. Miles Standish, we heard,
was not his second, but an unqualified third.

Emerging from an impoverished cultural life,
she aspired to emulate a legislator's wife.
As the square peg in a round hole,
she tried to envision what encompassed this role.

Opening those envelopes, my mother declares,
"It's formal! You know how that woman,
THE 'Mrs.' Miles Standish
puts on the airs."

My father dragged his black suit with tails
out of moth balls with the speed of a snail.
It aired for days, in the wind and sun,
reminder of their good times in Washington.

My mother failed to inquire how other's bones
would be covered, rightly presuming a formal scale.
When my parents arrived, my father alone
was clad in stiff white shirt, bowtie, and tails.

Red-faced, with barely suppressed moans,
they soon said goodbye to that high-columned home.
My father felt like Abraham Lincoln
arriving in Washington straight from a log cabin.

Never had I heard my father so adamant, so grim,
for my mother virtually dragging him
to her family's "occasion," one ever so hearty,
THAT "Mrs." Miles Standish's Cocktail Party.

2006

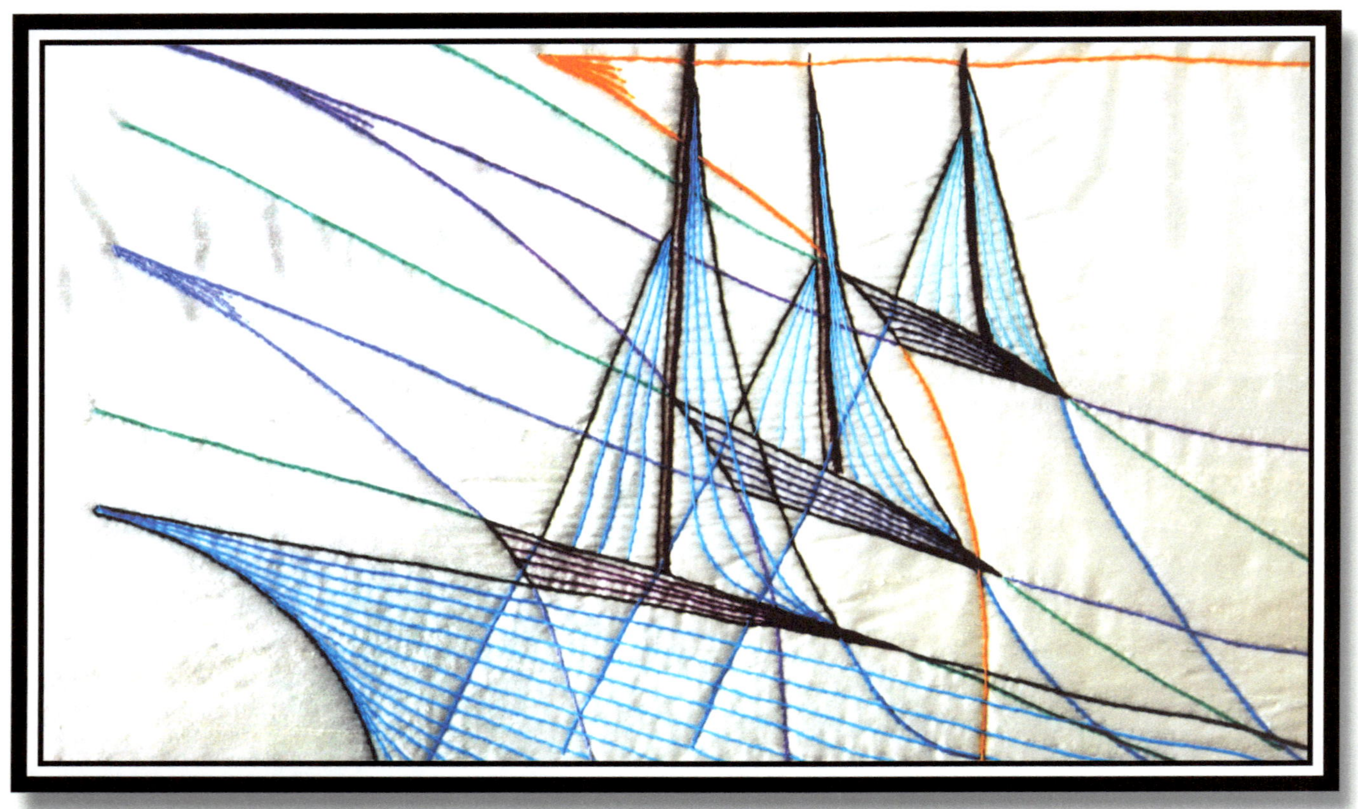

Ships Then and Now

Flax to Freedom

It is the **flax**

that's grown in fields
that's pulled in clumps
that's retted in pools
that's cracked to open
that frees the strands

— for spinning.

It is the **heddle**

that lifts the thread
that parts the warp
that moves the shuttle
that carries the woof
that is beaten firmly

— into cloth.

It is the **loom**

that women use
that weaves the linen
that makes the sails
that powers the ship
that carries the refugee

— to freedom.

1995

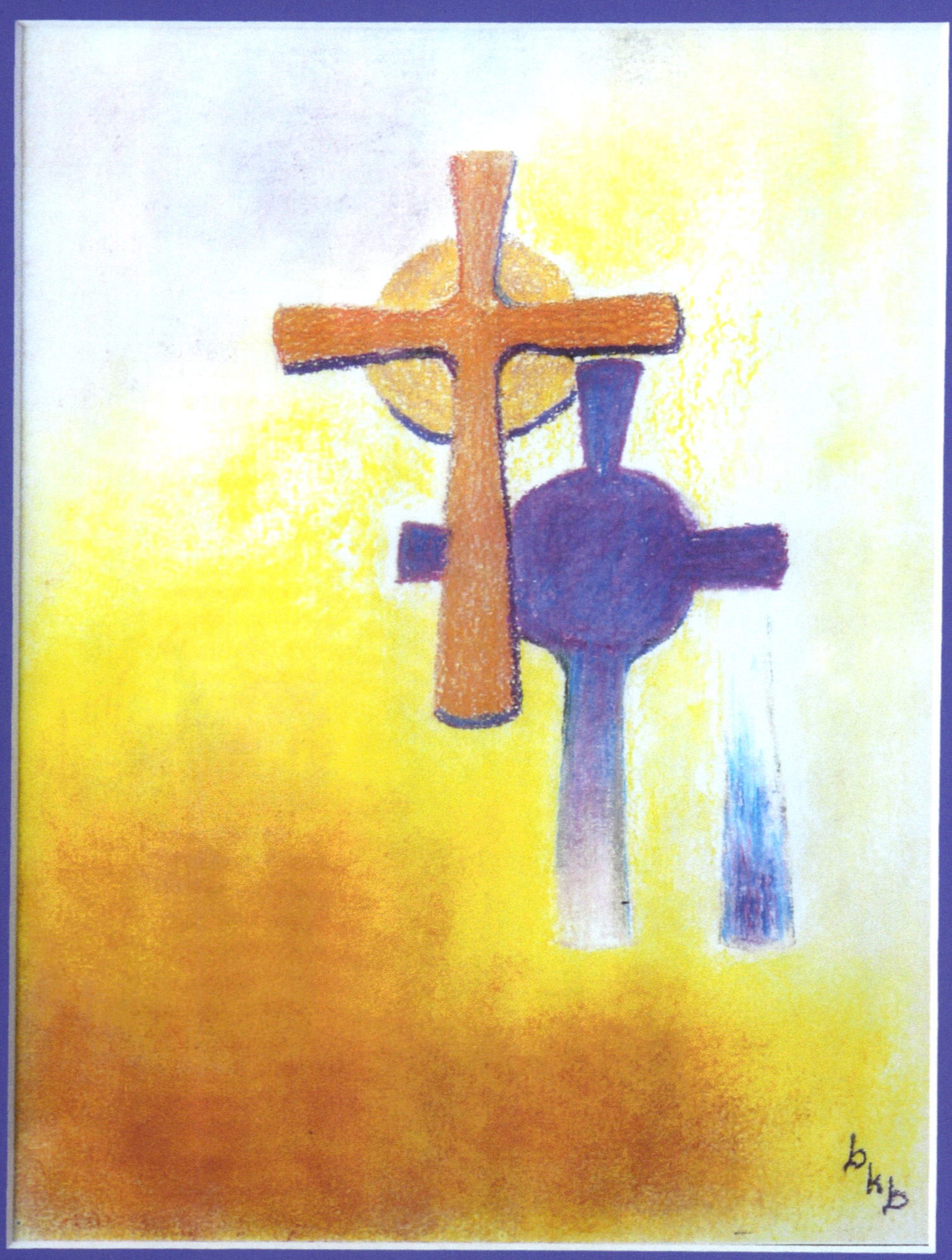

Wooden
Cross

Ode to Conradt Ham

Conradt, you are history for me.
You are my ancestor of deep, deep mystery.
You are my adventurous soul.
You are firm and constant, with a steadfast goal.
You are willing to explore life's risks to find.
Beside the Nahe that flows into the Rhine.

Like you, I explore the outreaches of my mind,
to learn from your history—hence it is mine.
When did they come, and where did they go?
It is traceable, definable, in the archives, though.

We share the land our footprints made.
We share the larch's spring-green shade.
We share their patterns against distant hill,
among forests of evergreens in the Palatines, still.

Conradt, you are history for me.
All the time I was stationed there,[1]
I knew not of the history we share.
It was two years for me,
a speck of time in history,
a homeland for you,
until you were twenty-two.
Along the Nahe that flows into the Rhine.

Generations before you, your family fled
the Catholics and the Second Spanish Inquisition,[2]
and instead,
they followed Erasmus, then Calvin's Reformist beliefs.
Under Spain's Duke of Alva they suffered torture and grief.

As Belgic Walloons, many fled to France,
absorbed by Huguenots to maintain their stance.
Eager Reformists, now Calvinists all,
generations later thousands fled old Gaul
to cross the Mosel to the bank of the Idar.

In the Palatines they were sheltered from pain.
They lived there as Protestants, their beliefs sustained.
As farmers, and cobblers, and sooted chimney sweeps,
they suffered when the Electors caused their taxes to
creep.
High above the Nahe that flows into the Rhine.

It was Britain's Queen Anne II in 1710
who offered you passage among three thousand men.
You were driven by taxes, and biting winter cold
to look for a new home and to better your soul.
Down the Nahe that flows into the Rhine.

Sailing from London, in ten ships strong,
across choppy seas in winter, all along,
to sail up the Hudson in search of pine, pitch, and tar,
to caulk ships of her navy that would fight wars afar.

You stepped ashore well north of Rhinebeck,
with family and home in mind, after your long trek.
Failure was certain on these river banks,
as hopes for enough pitch from these pine trees, sank.

Conradt, you are history for me.[3]
Unknown at the time I was stationed there,
or I would have begun my search for you, where…
where you, my ancestor of deep, deep mystery,
I learn only now, how we share the same history.
This is our Nahe that still flows into the Rhine.

1996

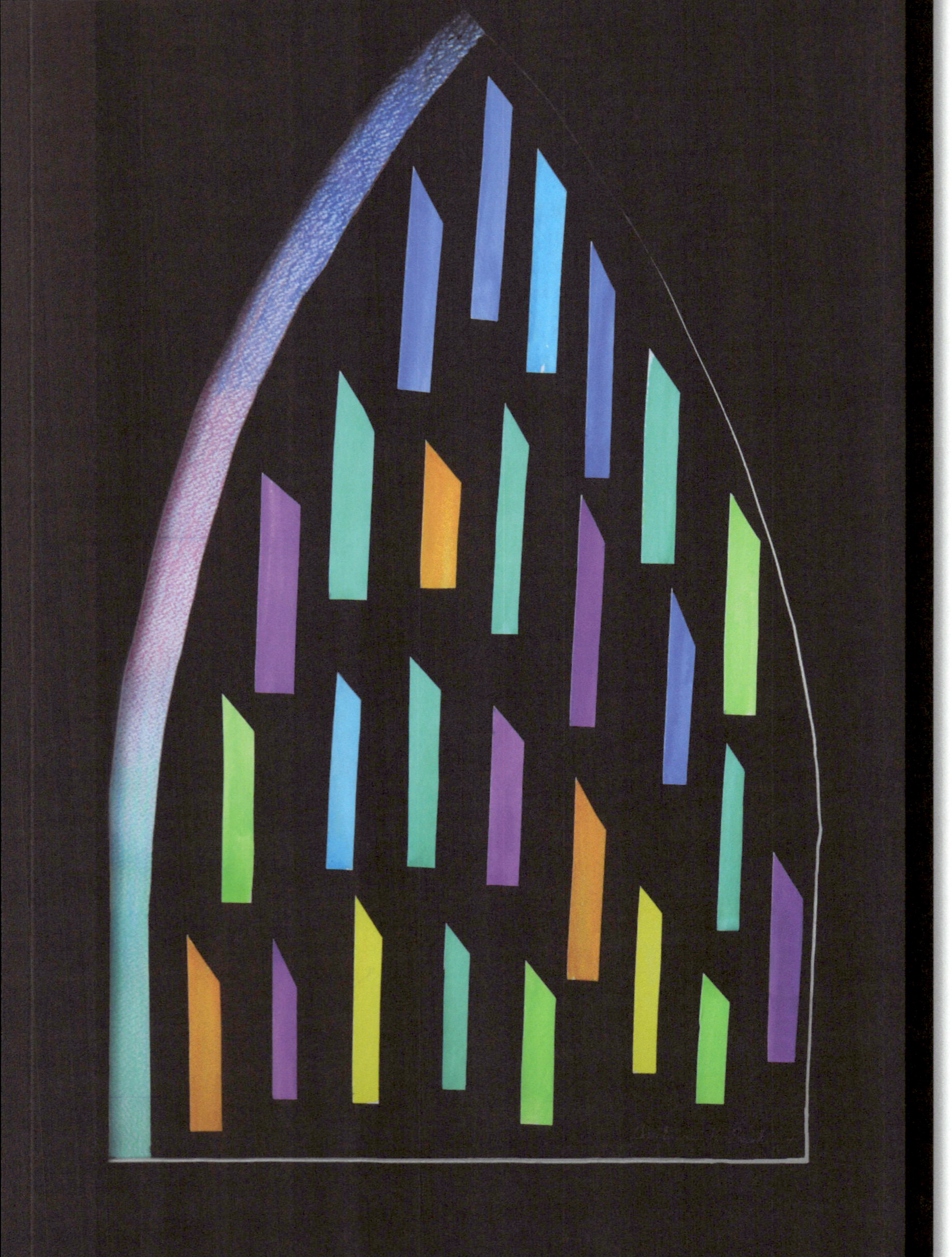

Arched Window

My Walloon Ancestors

I try to envision the courageous lives
those Walloon Reformists had led.
After first resisting, they fled to practice
their controversial beliefs instead.[1]

They fled to countries far and wide in fear
but mainly to Holland and France.
Generations later their descendants sailed here
to freedom, then met and married, by good chance.

Such is the tale of Adrian Vincent, child of Tournai[2]
whose family fled on the River Scheldt past Antwerp, to try
to seek refuge in Leyden. It was too crowded to stay,
so they sailed soon to London's unfettered gangway.

It would appear that in two generations or more,
a descendant by the same name
left for Nieuw Amsterdam[3] in 1634,
on the *Mary and John*, records maintain.[4]

Vincent descendants moved far upriver
to settle where the farmland was so much richer.
The Vincents and the Hams[5] became closely aligned.
Mary Vincent married Jonathan Ham in 1849.

Their first child was Eugene, who in 1881,
married Mary Kate Sleight and child number one
was Mary Ham who, in 1919, married my father
Harrie Doughty Knickerbocker.

2006

Ancestors of Choice

In twenty generations or more,
one's direct ancestors number in excess
of one million at the very core.

In searching family genealogy,
there is a strong proclivity of some
for preferential selection of one
or more, of notable detection,
prominent in science, history, or religion,
or a *Mayflower* passenger's adroit decision,
not as if it was "one in a million,"
but, as if that person symbolized
the whole centillion!

This leaves many of the rest
undistinguished, some boring at best.
Others, their generations knew,
were distinctly memorable
among close kin
for the questionable, self-serving tales
they could spin.

The psychopath, the embezzler, the gay—
I could cite a few, known in their day,
or those unmentionable woodpile relations,[1]
fully marginalized by families, sometimes.
They have every right to know the blood lines
from their ancestral plantation
as did the diverse descendants
of Thomas Jefferson's dark-skinned attendants.

Then there is the fugitive, Charles Germaine,[2]
an ancestor of mine who fled the iron chains
of La Tremblade Prison, in 1687,
south of his home in La Rochelle, hotbed
of Huguenot resistance, loyal Calvinists led.

His escape can be seen from two
diametrically opposed points of view.
The Papists condemned this as a dastardly act.[3]
The Calvinists lauded it as a daring feat,
so their religious beliefs might remain intact.

In America, Charles settled northward
of Boston in a village named New Orford.
A decade later he moved again, to join
other Huguenots from the French shoreline.
It comes as no surprise,
you can readily foretell,
they proudly named their spot
on the Hudson, New Rochelle.

2006

My Mind, My Reservoir

My mind, my reservoir for adventure,
adventure that is, in exploring the history
behind the events, the names and dates,
that provide a matrix for my family tree.

Adventure draws me
in one direction, then another,
to envision the picture of history
that looms much larger.
I recognize the traumas inflicted
upon my ancestors, those who
came from Belgium, Holland, France,
from Germany and England, too.

Then things changed.

Over here, many held fast
to their religious principles,
and their belief in the
rights of individuals.
On the other hand,
it is amazing to see
how quickly some lost
their ancestral memories.

The persecution their families
had endured,
they perpetrated on the next,
those hapless victims,
victims whose native land,
whose dress, whose customs, and beliefs
were soon decimated
by demand,

just as their own had been.

1996

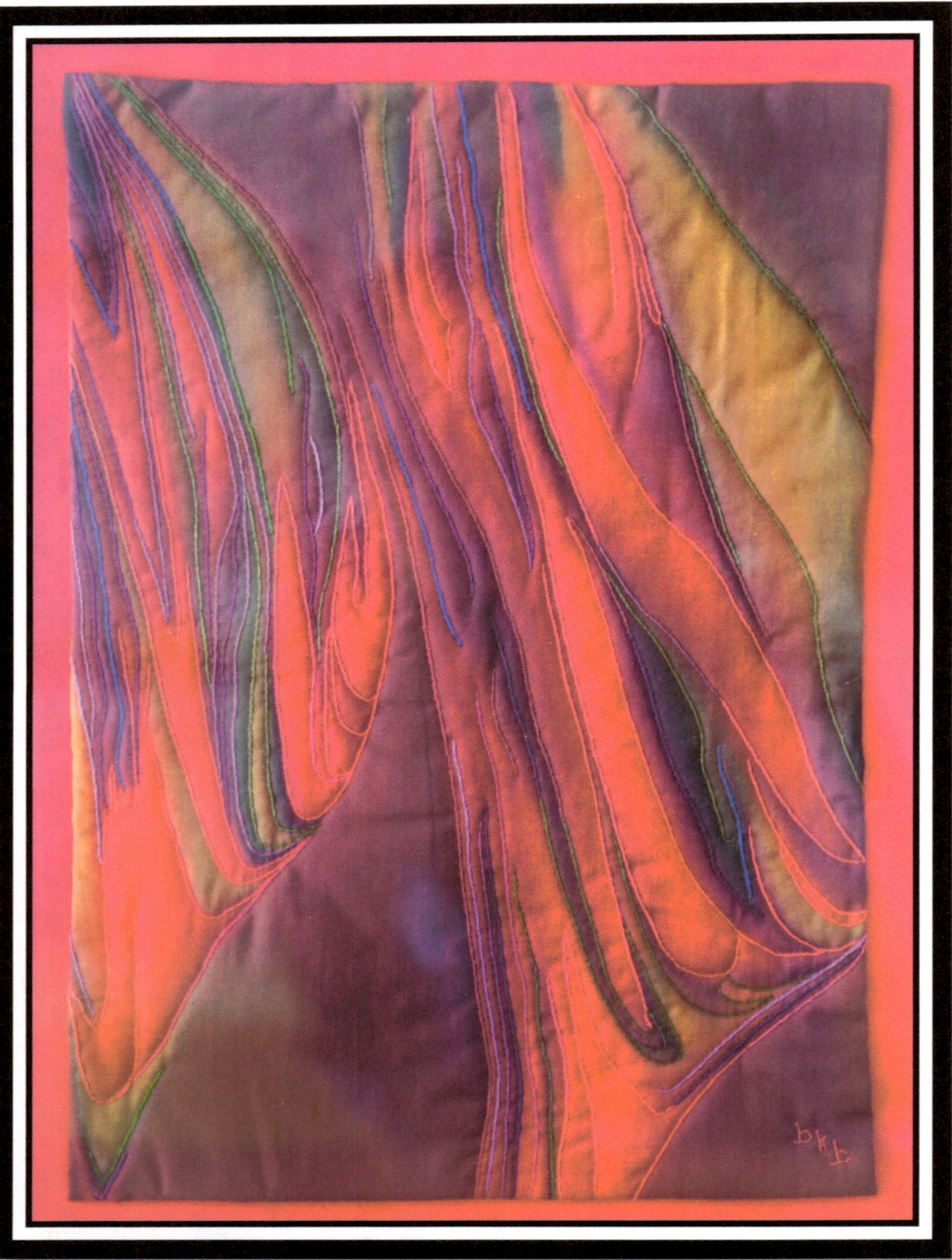

Sail into the Sunset

Poems

Part II

Mommy…

don’t leave me…

in this hostile house

alone.

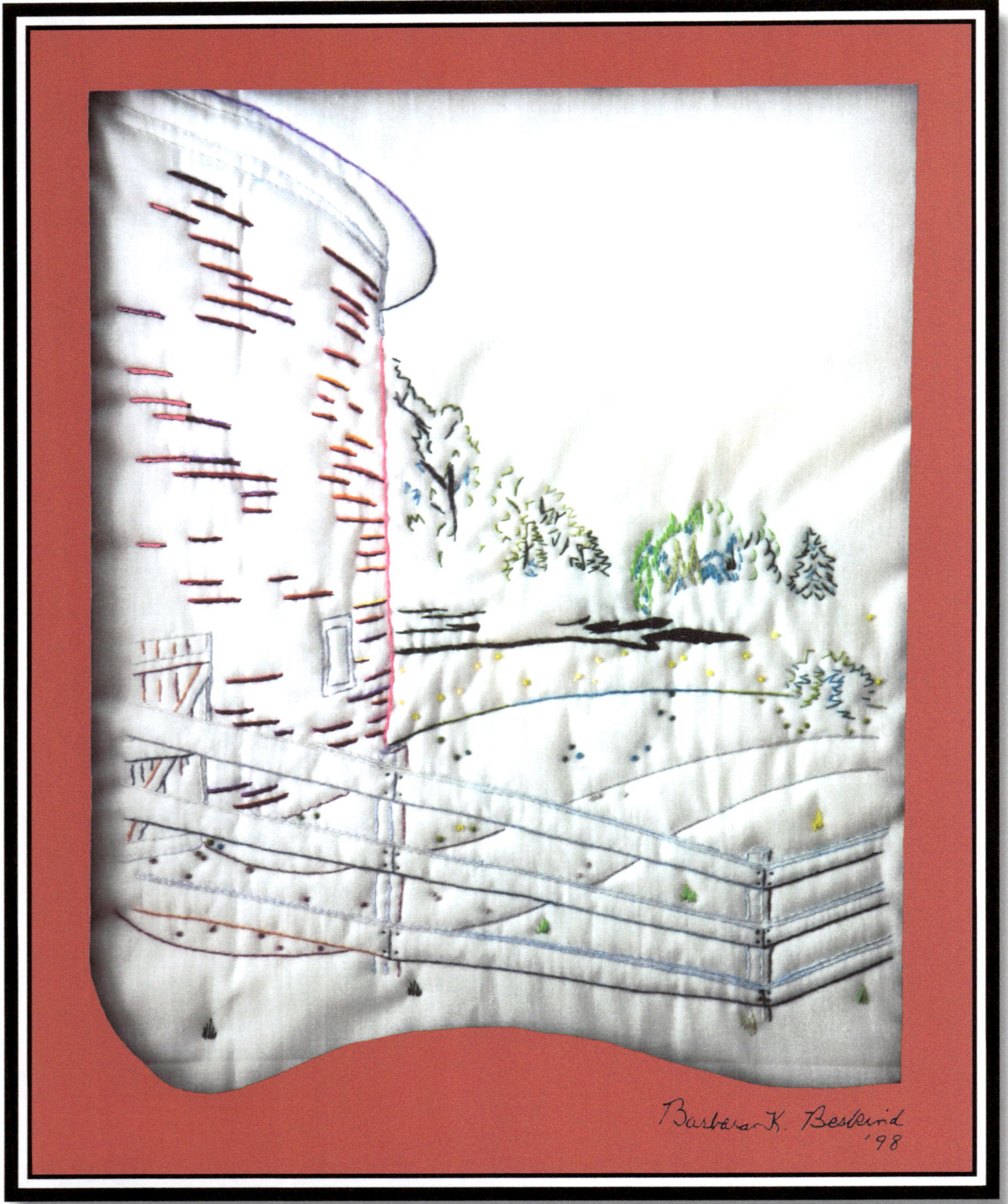

Round Barn at the Shelburne Museum

My Dear Grandparents

Grandma Ham, your name resounds with joy.
You acquired this name when you were married.
You and Grandpa had six children, and four
lived to adulthood to give you seven more.
How I envied my cousins, whose families of three
had sisters and a brother to share their glee.

You were sad never to hear our natural voices.
Squeals from your hearing aid scared us
when we were little. We grew curious
about how sounds into the speaker
attached to a battery and the cord in your ear
could bring a smile and, like magic, help you to hear.

We all knew, however, how much you loved us.
You had a gentle touch and gave us warm hugs.
On a shelf we could reach in the dining room cupboard,
you kept a cookie jar filled, unlike Mother Hubbard.
And you saved all the funny papers
of the *Herald Tribune.*

From Grandpa, stone-deaf for years,
there was a fond expression he had for us all.
When he said it, as inept as it may sound,
it unmistakably conveyed his affection.
"You're a stick-in-the-mud,"
he'd say with a straight face.

As little ones we'd wiggle, we'd giggle,
just as we did when he teased.
With his poker face, he'd playfully
interact the best way he could,
poking us with the tip of his cane just as he
poked the cows into their stanchions for milking.

After nearly sixty years of mutual devotion
their wordless interaction needed only a motion.
A glance, a gesture, a tender pat on the shoulder
spoke volumes about their long lives together.
Bonded in life, they fully expected
to be united once more in the long hereafter.

2006

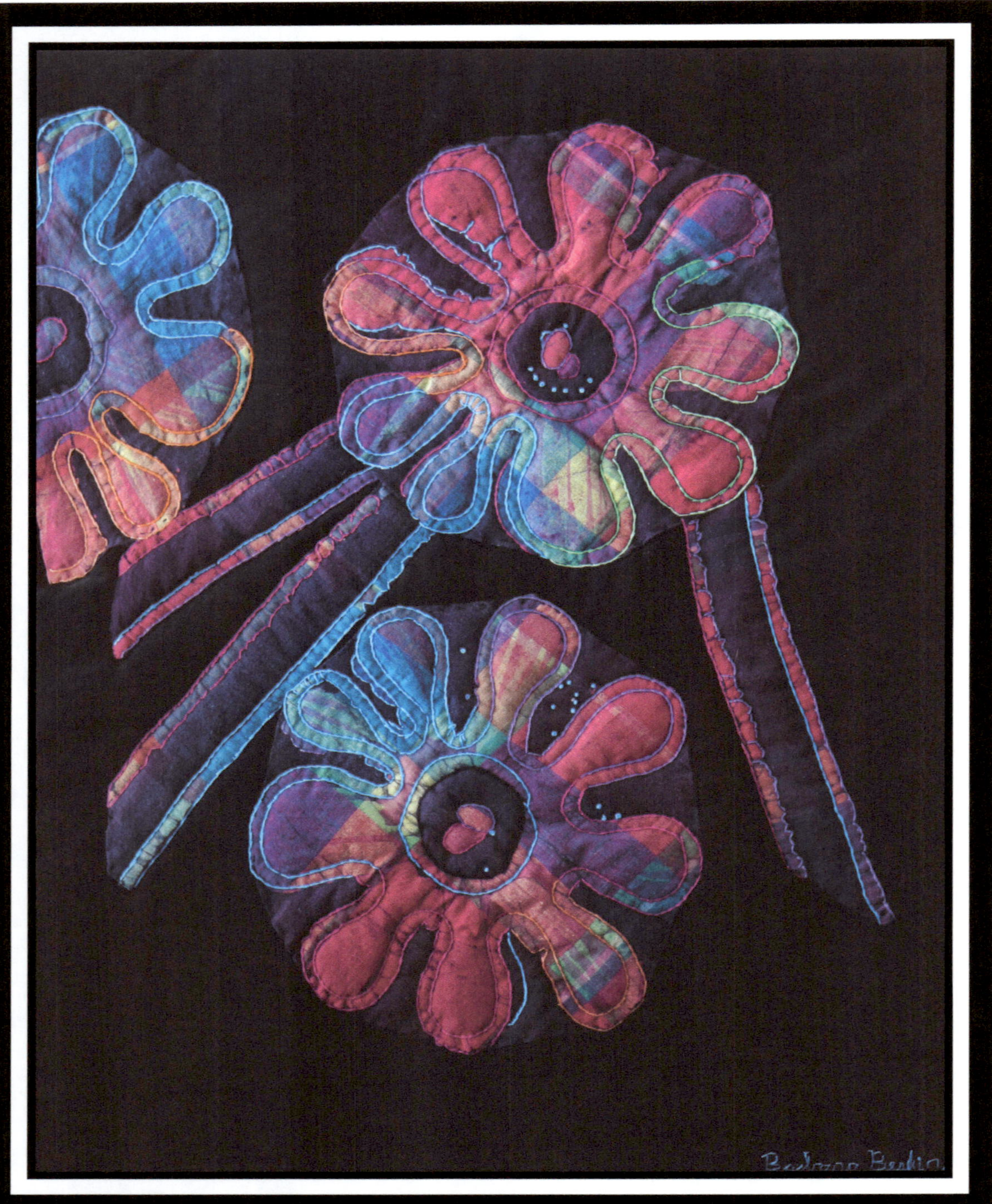

Poppies by Design

Letter to Grandma "K."

Amid flowers in my garden, I'll stay all day.
It's here in Vermont, I write to you, Grandma "K."[1]
During the big "D" Depression,
your little "d" depression went unrecognized.
Could we have done more about it, had we realized?

You kept yourself contained, unexposed, like living in—
inside an egg from our Plymouth Rock hens.
We couldn't reach you, felt rejected when we tried.
I was frightened. I thought you didn't like me inside—
because I was a child.

I kept out of sight and was ever so quiet.
I listened, I watched, and learned all I was able,
by creating my home under the living room table.
From silence and strain, peace could quickly erode.
Your house seemed like a powder keg about to explode.

And yet, beneath your shell there must have been
a person I wanted to know.
To write you now makes me sad enough to cry.
I want to cry out to you, to ask
for answers unspoken, to understand at last.

Who was the person Grandpa knew and surely
must have loved, when both of you were young?
What happened that made you close the door
and bolt it from within? In your Victorian house,
was there a well-locked secret amid three floors?

Or, did your intellectual yearning seem so demanding
to incite your withdrawal, your anger notwithstanding?
Did your brilliant mind haunt you, demand more instead?
Did Wordsworth, Shelley, Shakespeare, and Keats
gratify you more than Grandpa's gracious treats?

Were you deeply jealous of this merchant's goodwill,
idolized by townspeople, of whom he never thought ill?
Was it his warmth, his good humor, his generosity to a fault?
Those traits were so human, you were unable to relate.
What made life rich for him, was hard for you to contemplate.

When he died, wasn't there some way to have grieved your loss,
some way to have expressed it beside your austere façade,
and your cloistered aloofness from public promenade?
Was it our very presence that reminded you,
of impending closure, on your life's journey, too?

Instead of personal warmth for me, you placed your affinity
with public causes, to the Democratic Party,
in defense of our country with a big "D" Democracy.
Maybe you also applauded democracy with a little "d,"
for those beyond the rigid, frigid walls in which we lived.

~

I've been thinking of you, Grandma "K.,"
amid flowers in my garden, where I spend the day.
I remember your garden well, the one beside
the lilac bush that shaded from the road
the square, old outhouse, primitive and cold.

With the same regularity of your coming downstairs
to listen to news at noon about foreign affairs
would be the annual appearance of California poppies.
Tangerine petals cupped stamens of black
on plants big as our washtub, each year they came back.

They peeped over the mound of our well-cut lawn,
visible from the house and the roadway beyond.
Bachelor buttons, straight-stemmed and blue,
flowing clusters of white daisies shot up, too.
How they loved the hot sun and showers in the afternoon.

~

It is here in my garden, in Vermont, Grandma "K.,"
I am closest to you, and for the first time, I can say
I feel your presence in my life—with joy.
I use your garden tools, the narrow rake, the trowel,
whose splinter-free handles helped grind your hardened soil.

I found the "claw" hand rake with the handle Grandpa extended—
attached with sturdy wire, now rusted, from years untended—
so with more ease, your frail arms could reach,
from that tiny, five-foot body reach, out—
if not to human beings, to close generations of garden weeds.

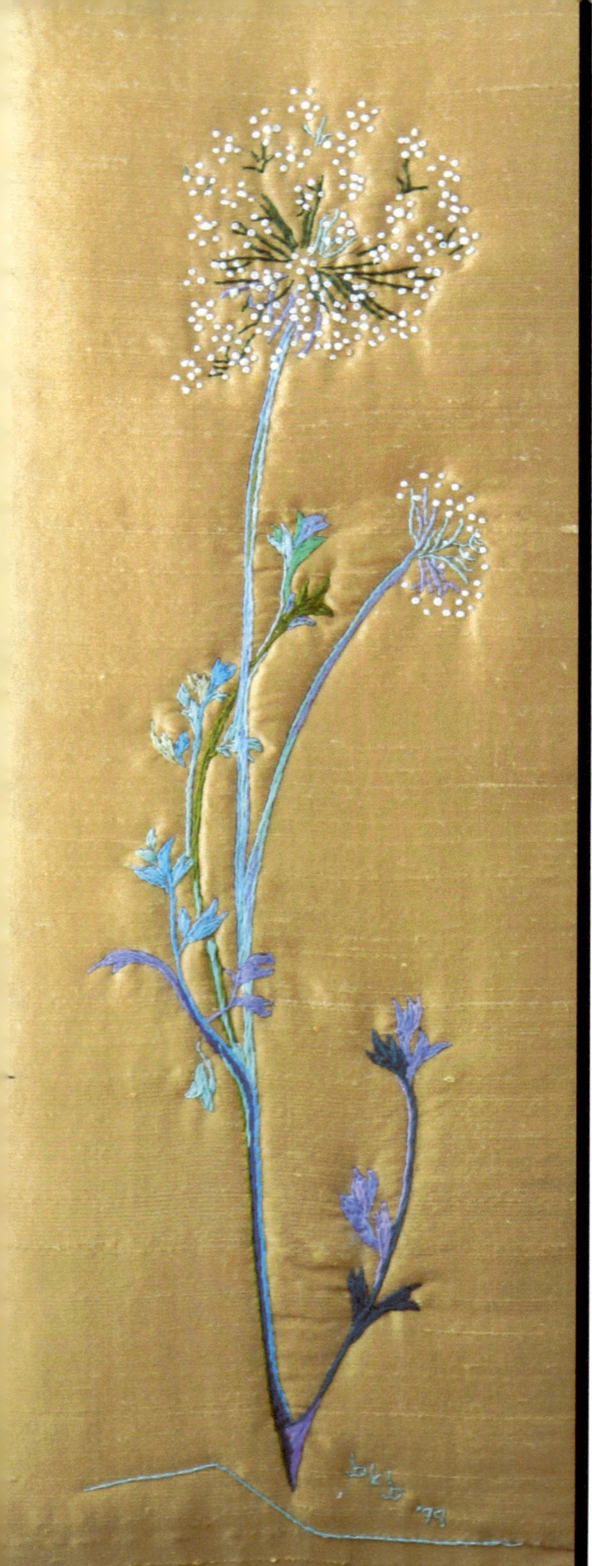

I remember how, with sweat pouring down your tissue-paper
cheeks, you would work hard, with bare hands to dig, to rake
throughout the steamy summer mornings, without a break.
We worried you might overdo, you and the heat, both ninety-two.
But our concern was for naught—you scarcely noticed 'til noon.

It seemed to me, when you weeded your garden,
you were closest to enjoying yourself. You were unguarded.
Perhaps it was therapeutic for you, as it is for me,
close to mother nature's magnetic force to be.
That unseen force—now pulls us together from far, far apart.

You never allowed us to share your experience,
to witness serenity, or real joy in your life.
If only you could have, it would have eased our strife.
Permission to enjoy ourselves, as grandchild, son, and daughter-in-law—
to share more of our lives with you—required a deep spring thaw.

I longed for a more traditional, affectionate relationship
as grandchild to grandparent, but our love stayed un-kindled.
Now I feel some heritage through my garden flowers.
I, too, grow California poppies, and hollyhocks that tower
above bachelor buttons and wild, white daisies like yours.

I am content when I grasp the tools you used so long,
those tools we might have shared, if you had cared.
I can be closer to you in my garden than ever
I could have been, watching from the sidelines, for never
would you speak as you worked in your garden—alone.

These tools are a legacy that bind us, among those
very few things I preserved from your house, because
this was always your house, your home, never ours, never mine.
Now we can share those flowers your tools help to blossom.
This bond makes it better for us both, better for my mind.

I am, with all the best wishes I can find,

Your distant relative, and granddaughter,

Barbara

2003

Queen Anne's Lace

Alternate Saga

(during the impeachment hearings of President Clinton)

Little Rock took a tumble.
Momma Boxer consoles,
Pappa Lieberman scolds
for his being so clumsy.

Embarrassed, Grandpa Bird
looks down, and comments over
his grandson's behavior
before all the Elders:

"Don't you know this island's
Constitutional By-Laws?"
Red-faced Henry Hyde
is mad as a hatter.

Behind, Dale Bumpers chides:
"None of us is perfect…remember, Henry?"
"Don't be too hard on Little Rock….
Someday, we too may fall."

1999

Author's Note: Given Grandma "K's" unfettered allegiance to the Democratic Party, especially to FDR, it could make good theatre, were we able to watch her response six decades later. It might challenge unquestioned support of another President from the Democratic Party.

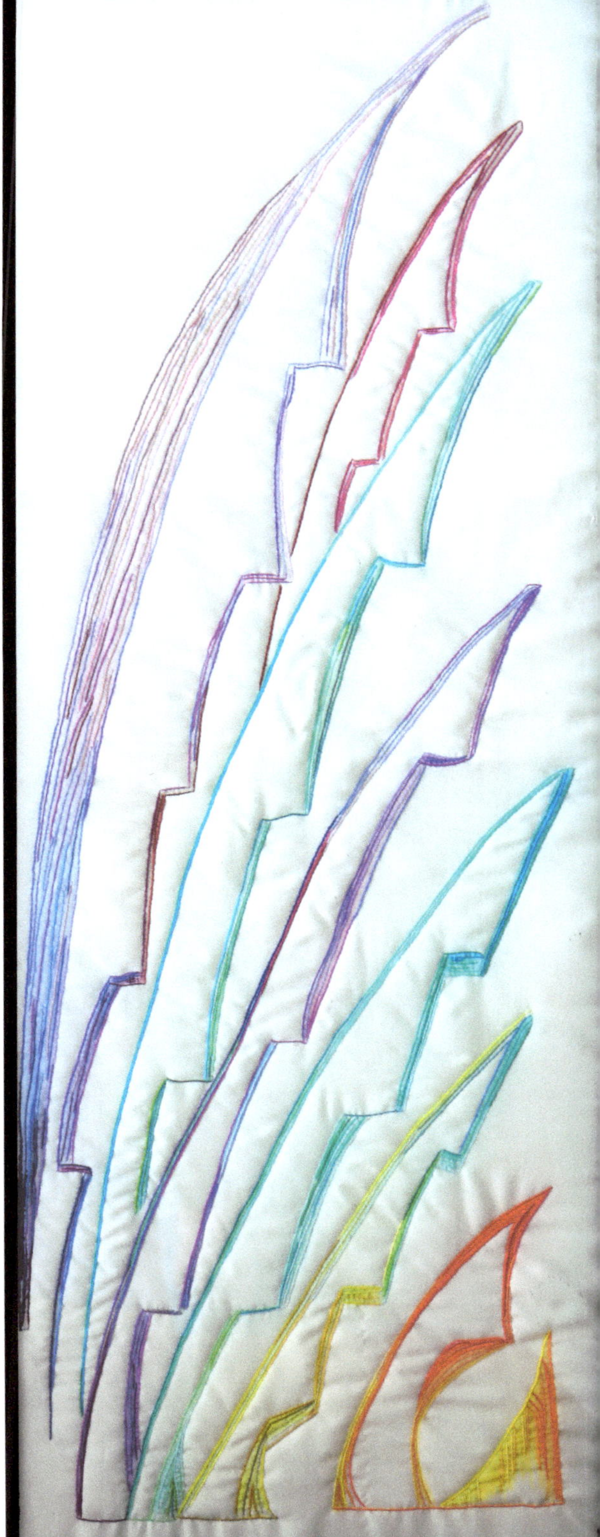

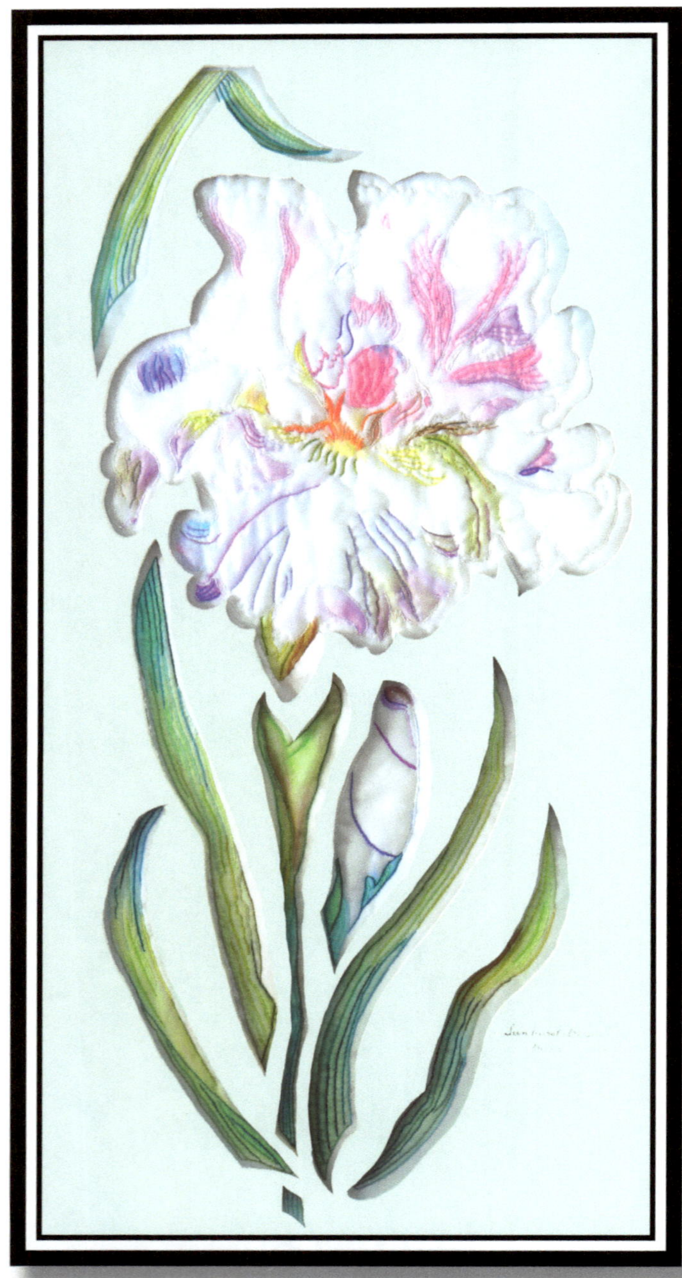

White Iris

Smiley

I am the grocer of my soul.
I take bread off the grocery shelf
to put the freshest loaves at the back.
I date the "milk of life"
for safe consumption.

Emotions can't be weighed
on the scale in Grandpa's store,
but feelings toward Grandma,
like un-refrigerated milk,
could soon turn sour.

Long after her death at ninety-six,
pictures of her are carved in stone
like statues on Easter Island.
Never did I see a crack.
I rename her "Smiley."

1996

FOUR

I wished as a child there were four of us.
How desperately I wanted a baby brother
to replace the one before me
who died at birth without another.
Had he lived, they would perhaps have heeded
the doctor's advice to have no more,
my mother then nearly forty-four.
He shook his head and said, "Too risky."
First she smiled, and then without
a second thought replied briskly,
"I'll take my chances."
Or I would never have been born.

1996

Naptime of a Three-Year-Old

Mommy! Mommy! Are you asleep?
Don't leave me here.
Don't die! Wake up!
Don't leave me hostage
in this hostile house,
alone.

1996

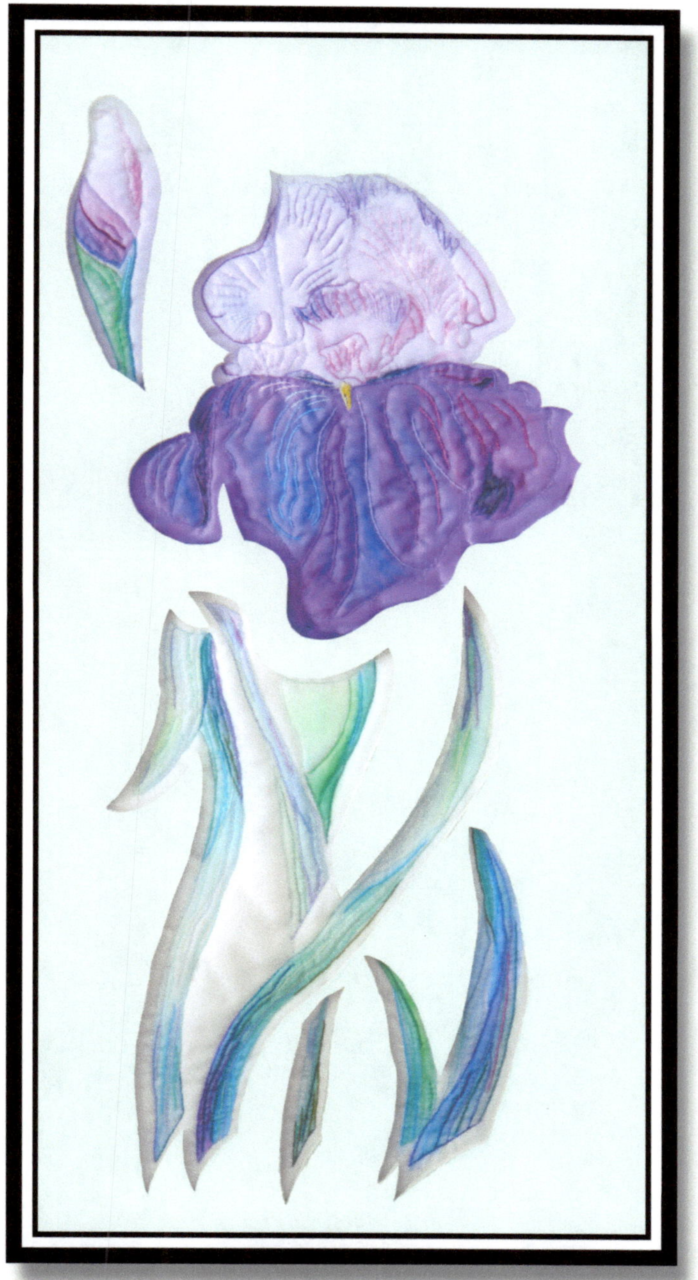

Purple Iris

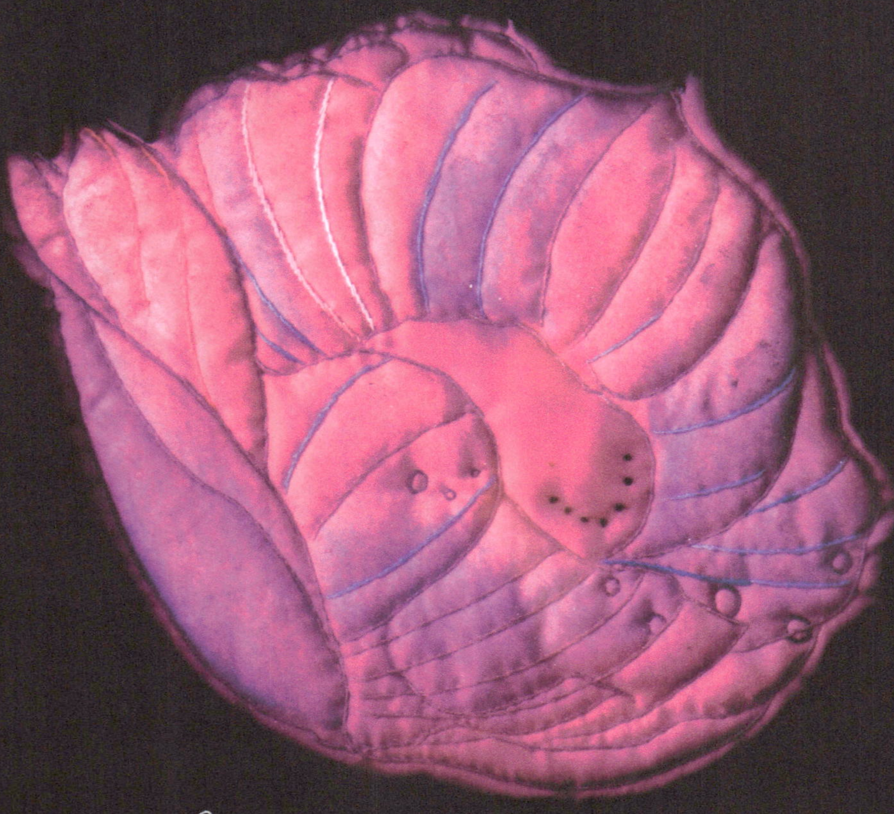

Ruby Anemone

A Line of Time in Eternity

Looking back at my childhood,
the two people I was closest to,
were my mother and Grandma Ham,
her mother I saw too infrequently.

Those visits were so treasured
and the pinnacle each year
was the party for this grandmother
who was born on New Year's Day.

The year my mother was eighty
I watched her struggle valiantly
in order not to pass away on Christmas
and dampen future years of celebrations.

Although I had deep affection for my father, too,
I never remember the date when he died in October,
nor am I ever reminded of his mother's demise,
on Armistice Day, when hostilities ceased.

I recall my mother's death so vividly,
when cancer claimed that brave one.
It was precisely at ten minutes of ten
on New Year's Eve.

Never in these ensuing forty-five years
has New Year's Eve arrived that I have
not had immediate recollections of her life,
her passing, and the impact of her life on mine.

The two people so close to each other
and so close to me, were born and died
each side of the calendar line of time,
that line of time in eternity.

2006

Then and Now

Then it was rare…almost unheard of:

I never knew anyone, who

had cancer

until 1962

when my mother died.

Now it is just as rare…it is unheard of:

for anyone who does not know

a loved one, friend or neighbor, who

has died,

is in treatment for,

or among the many like me

to have been cured.

2006

Poems

Part III

Earthquakes

in time

and space

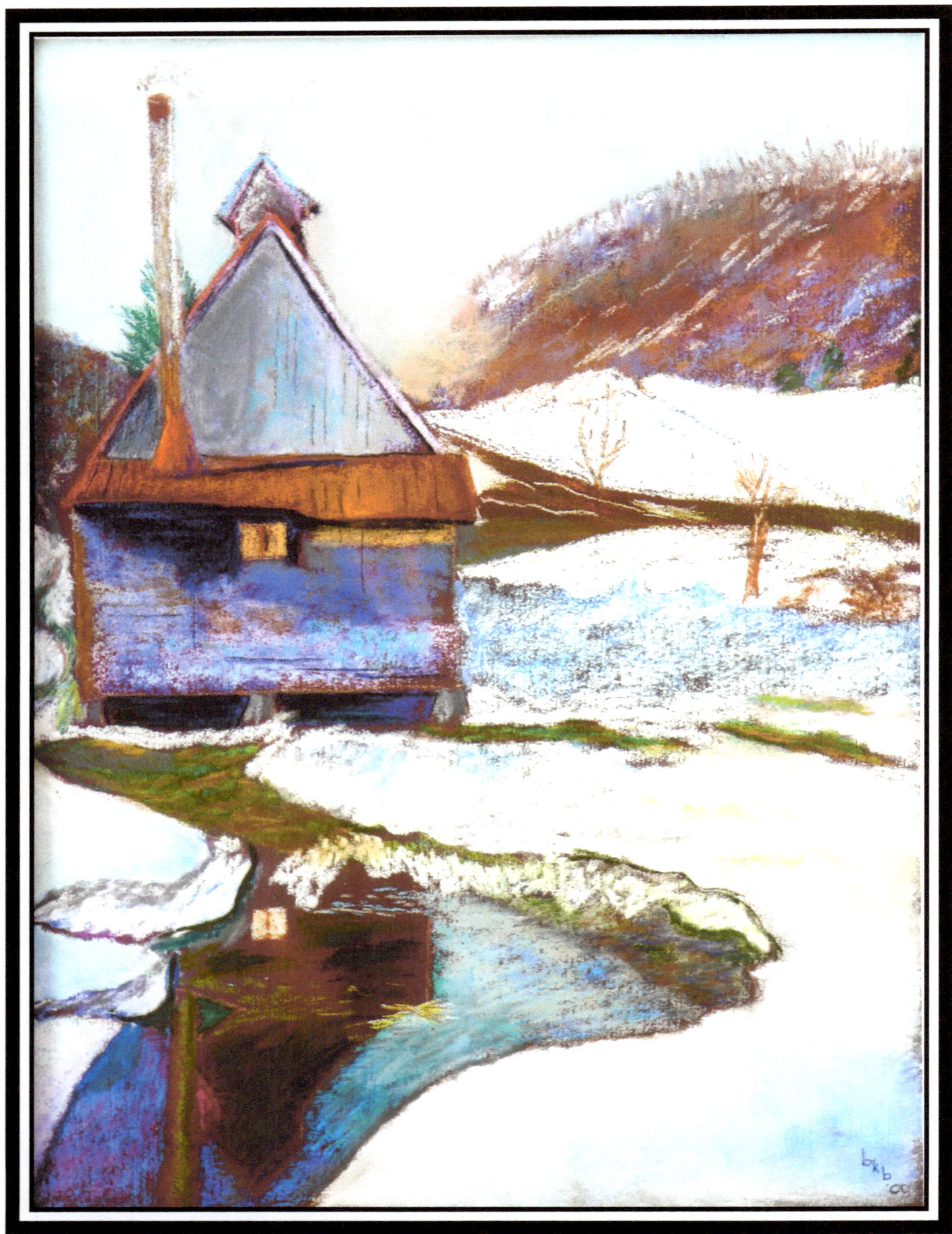

Vermont Sugar House

Altered Perceptions

For Alzheimer's Disease there is no known cure
but following the long trail to the end, I am sure

there are moments, or insights, of the loved one's experience
that bring a unique perspective, one often at variance.

For the afflicted, this may appear as a resolution or relief,
to the caregiver, a moment of humor, both sad and brief.

Such was the time our golden retrievers ran off.
Loving Vermont's "mud season" they rolled in every trough.

Following Sugarbush, Pied Piper of the crew
were Big Ben Beskind and Muffins, mother of those two.

Gone for days, along roads, woods, and trails,
I drove miles looking, listening, and calling to no avail.

I stopped every UPS truck, mailman, and jogger,
implored them for news and gave them our number.

I put it on the radio and waited by the phone,
then set out again when someone unknown

reported they were scrounging for food,
at a muddy logging camp, far distant and crude.

By the time I reached there, long gone were they.
Tails a-wagging, they had trotted on their merry way.

Beside me in the car my mother-in-law sensed then
how anxious I was, fearful I'd never see them again.

In her altered perception, to placate my fears,
said: "Barbara, if everyone you'd asked here

brings you a dog, you'd have hundreds."
I replied, "Mom, you're certainly right."

But to feed them, keep them all penned,
and then buy dog tags—"Oh, what a plight!"

I just wanted to see our frolicsome three, and then
after four days came word of the females and "Big Ben."

A Vermont housewife phoned to ask me whether
these were ours, saying, they were lying together

in the morning on their long, dirt road,
more than ten miles from their own abode.

I jumped in the car and sped there immediately,
to thank her. I agreed they were exhausted—and filthy.

The Pied Piper, too tired to jump into the Volvo was she.
Muddy as they were, we welcomed them with glee.

Thankfully it was just these three we would be keeping penned
and fed, in hopes this fiasco would not happen again.

2005

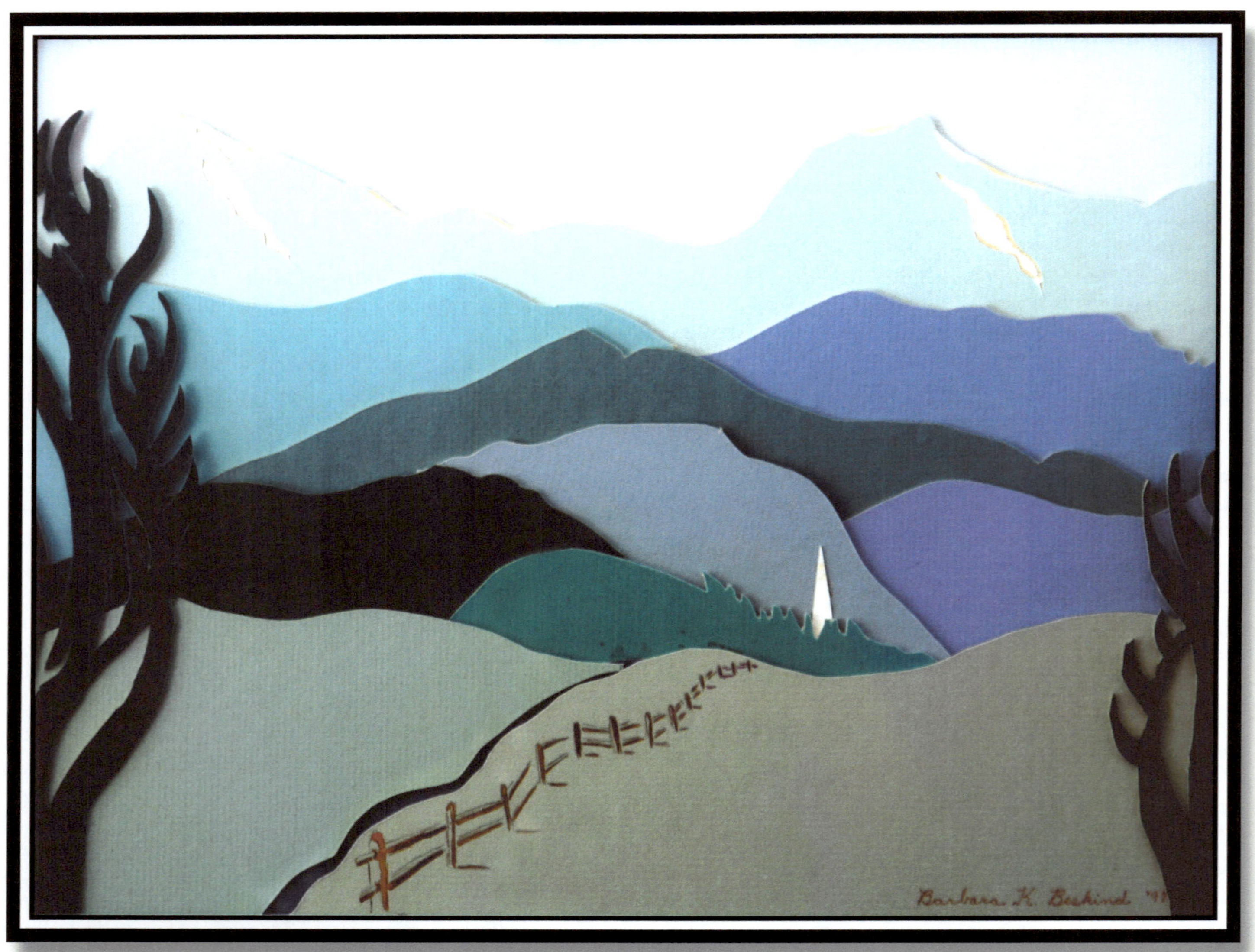

Green Mountains of Vermont

Our Last Journey

With her Alzheimer's advancing at a steady pace
I look back at our last journey as a memorable space.

As long as I had known my mother-in-law, what we enjoyed best
was to go shopping, to laugh, to explore, and to invest

in new clothes for her which I could alter to fit,
or she could help me select my new outfit.

We could still enjoy this last shopping trip, a stop
on our way to the airport in Burlington, Vermont.

It was before her mind closed in beyond our reach then.
She could still travel by plane, a family member at each end.

On this hundred-mile trip along the interstate, on-coming lanes
were often above, or below, us or behind rocks, all the same.

Mom's comment to me was: "I don't see why
they need these roads. Not a car has come by

the other way as long as you've been driving."
Thankfully none faced us to prevent our safe arriving.

This was our last journey, and in good measure
I can reflect on it with comfort and pleasure.

2005

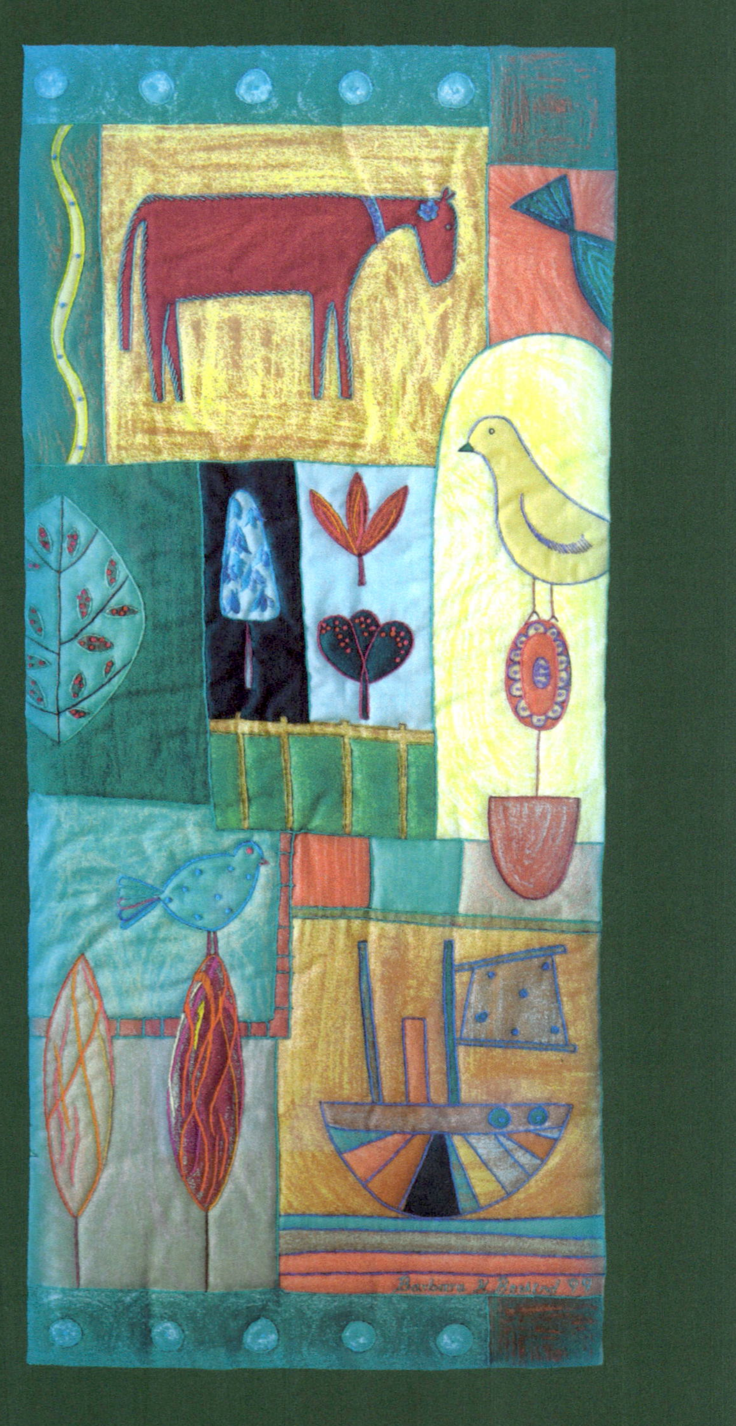

Vermont History in the Abstract

Earthquakes in Vermont

Earthquakes happen fast in time and space,
but Vermont seems such an unlikely place.

Sudden upheavals create an unexpected jolt.
My first experience nearly caused me to bolt.

A fault-line stretches from above Montreal,
down the Connecticut River, far below Bellows Falls.

Another couple was entertaining us at a private occasion.
We sampled our hotel-host's impressive wine collection.

He had proudly displayed the wine cellar downstairs
where he preserved his finest for their fancy affairs.

Barely seated, we unfolded our napkins, then gave a toast.
Nearest the kitchen, I sniffed the aroma of the chef's rib-roast.

From a jarring jolt to the back of my chair,
I envisioned a clumsy waiter stumbling there.

We stared. "Tingling goblets shake and shake!"
In disbelief we gasped the word: *"earthquake!"*

Our host dashed to the cellar with the distinct aim
to see if his wines warranted an insurance claim.

He had just boasted being among those very few who
carried "earthquake insurance" Vermonters pooh-poohed.

He found each bottle intact in its very own cradle,
as the waiter waited, with hot soup to be ladled.

The next quake in Vermont was of longer duration.
Its vivid image produced a most memorable configuration.

Before I realized what was happening to me innermost
my cat dashed down the hillside as if chased by a ghost!

In the next instant I sensed as well as I was able,
the sun's reflection above the glass coffee table.

A sharp contour crossed the ceiling back and forth,
swaying like a pendulum from south to north.

While frozen in fright, I committed to memory
a shape of abstract beauty, an artistic discovery.

This dramatic impression of earth's power to shift
from the known, to the unknown, was alarmingly swift!

Like earthquakes occurring in time and space,
marriages too can be disrupted any time, any place.

This earth-shaking trauma amid life's stores
is a reality few have the luxury ever to ignore.

2006

Trees of Sorrow ... Trees of Joy

The car glides to a stop at the usual spot for me to think,
to reflect on my therapy and to sip a drink.

In cold silence I grasp the coffee cup, hot, and listen
to the jingle of rings, while frosted still glisten.

Transferred now to the other hand, my cherished solitaire
reflects our seventeen years as a well-bonded pair.

My throat tightens, I cannot swallow. I can scarcely see
through the blurred windshield at shimmering trees.

Never have I liked dull, drab oak leaves.
I prefer Vermont's orange, yellow, and red-maple seas.

"Look, there's a bright maple…cuddled among the oaks."
I cry out, but no one is there to hear. My cheeks are soaked.

Dry oak leaves match our walnut and teak
closer than the oak flooring now somber and bleak.

A spectrum of wild, weird, and vivid associations
burst from my mind in multiple variations.

Beside distant pasture walls majestic oak trees match
Gurnseys and Jerseys near a thorny "black" berry patch.

Dew-covered oaks resemble cold copper, bronze, and brass
as vibrant color drains from the maples, poplars, and ash.

The "oohs" and "ahs," and camera clicks are gone. Loaded
busses, vans, and tourists' cars no longer roam back roads.

The corn is cut. The leaves are raked. Pumpkins line our drive.
Wood is stacked in garrison-piles, its warmth alone I'll derive.

Autumn is different for me this year; it is for others, too.
Our summer was dry, the foliage dull, in winter's drab preview.

The sumac's lack of scarlet hues embodies my disappointment.
Cinnamon-colored oaks reflect fall's image, now so imminent.

Leaves trickle down like tears to blanket yards and landscapes
    from wall to stonewall, rail fence to wire, back roads to interstates.

Along the Connecticut River Valley, my sensations are so magnified.
    October sun drills against my shoulder, its fiery warmth intensified.

Associations are sparked from glossy leaves
    and endless shades of roadside trees.

My imagination is tugged, released, then springs
    like a nimble marionette pulled by taut strings.

A stand of oaks wraps farthest hills in nature's soft allure,
    like church-pew cushions enveloped in bronze velour.

Evergreens surround the reds and purples in autumn awe,
    converting Mt. Ascutney into a giant paisley shawl.

Closer to home the four-lane highway shrinks to two,
    black-top turns to dirt. I pass our house to search the view

from the timber road which tapers to a rocky path
    and terminates beside the fire tower shaft.

In slow rhythm I trudge up one step at a time,
    listening for his familiar footstep aligned with mine.

Alone I scan that landscape at dusk
    the one that had been bright has turned to rust.

Memories are defined by both time and space.
    The trips with bikes and mountain hikes took place

amid the lavenders and pinks of those far-away peaks
    that resound still with the joy of yesterday's retreats.

1996

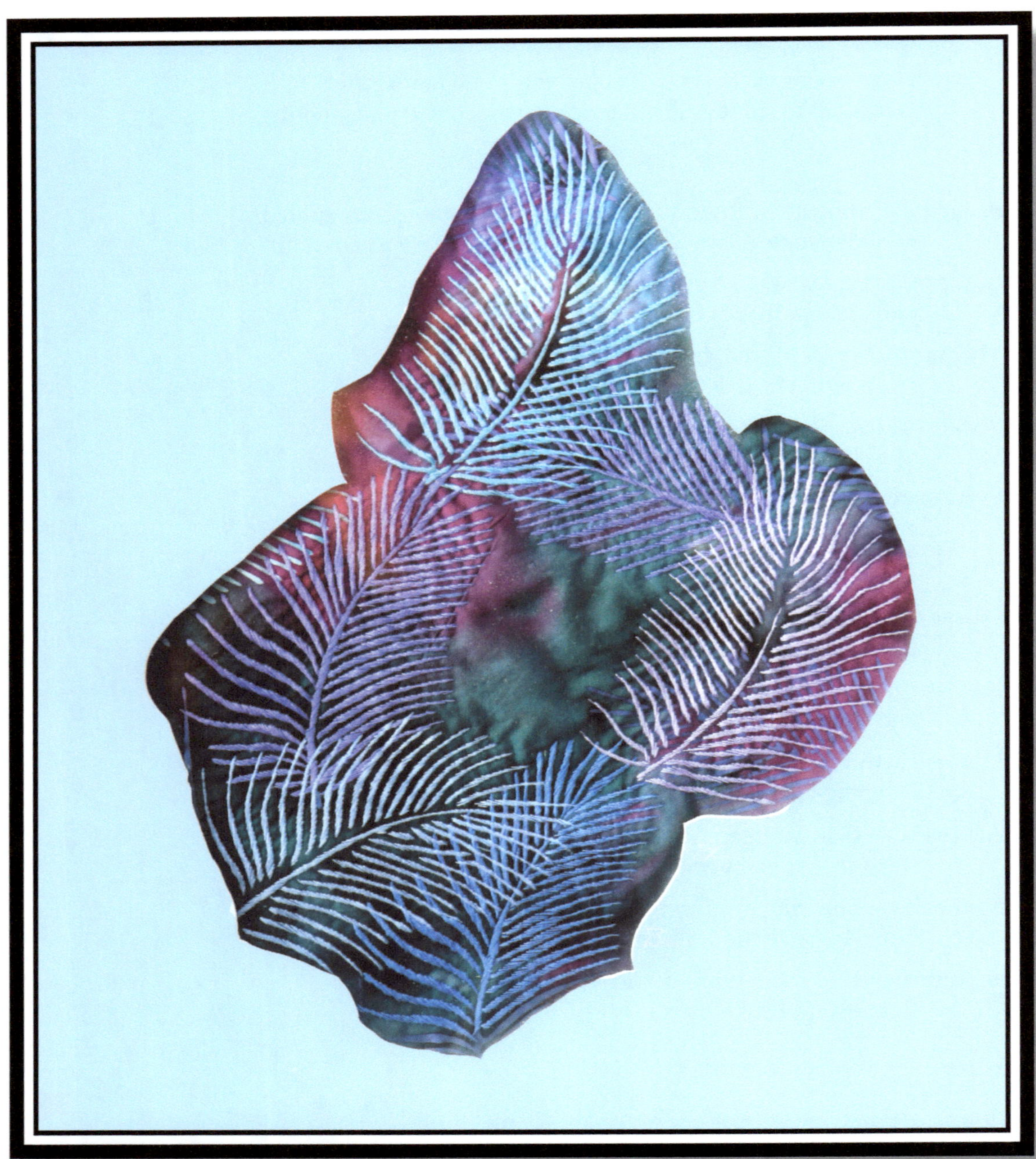

Blue Spruce

You Were, You Are

You were my rock, my lion, my sponge,
acknowledging my needs and responding
in softness, empathy, respect, and love.
Your needs changed and so did mine.

You needed my support
to soothe, to tame your anxieties.
We needed to explore broader interests
of things we could do together.

Now, you are my concerned other, my friend
to back up my fledgling efforts
to balance a checkbook, pay the bills,
make sure the car is roadworthy.

You are respectful of my endeavors,
you trust and encourage me in my new life
and I just want to say:

Thank you for being,

    if not for me

        for someone else —

            whom you deserve

                to do for you

                    what I could not.

1996

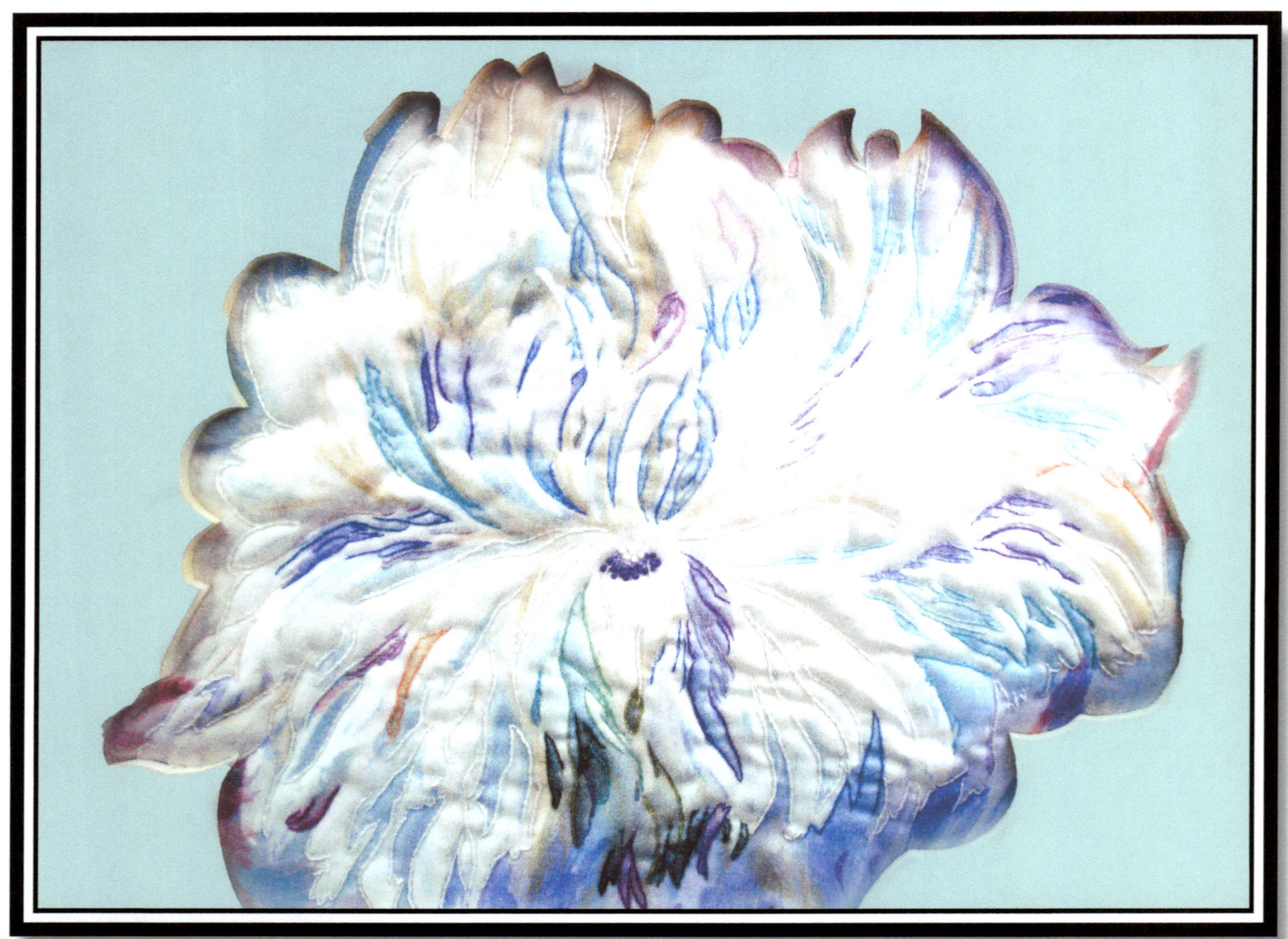

Peony for Diana

It is Over

It is over now,
but can that ever be?
Memory doesn't fade,
doesn't lose its vivid color.
Like watercolors in midday light
are the memories of a past delight--
the touch of your hand upon my shoulder,
faith you would be here as we grew older.

It is no more.
I won't trespass,
I won't invade
that life that is yours today.
I could disrupt your peace
in ways we know and share.
I won't. I have too many feelings
for me not to care.

I cannot let the fact you chose
another path in life
govern, or detract, from mine.
I have found creative alternatives.
At first none were superlatives,
but I have developed a rich, viable life
nourished by the memories
of a satisfied time, a gratified life with you.

1996

Tunneling Out

In these past few years
I've been deep down under
tunneling beneath the riverbed
below the Hudson River
digging my own version of the Holland Tunnel
with only a teaspoon in hand
when I really needed a front-end loader.
Now that I am near the other end
I have the energy of an earthmover.
I find life is lighter and brighter
on the other side.

1996

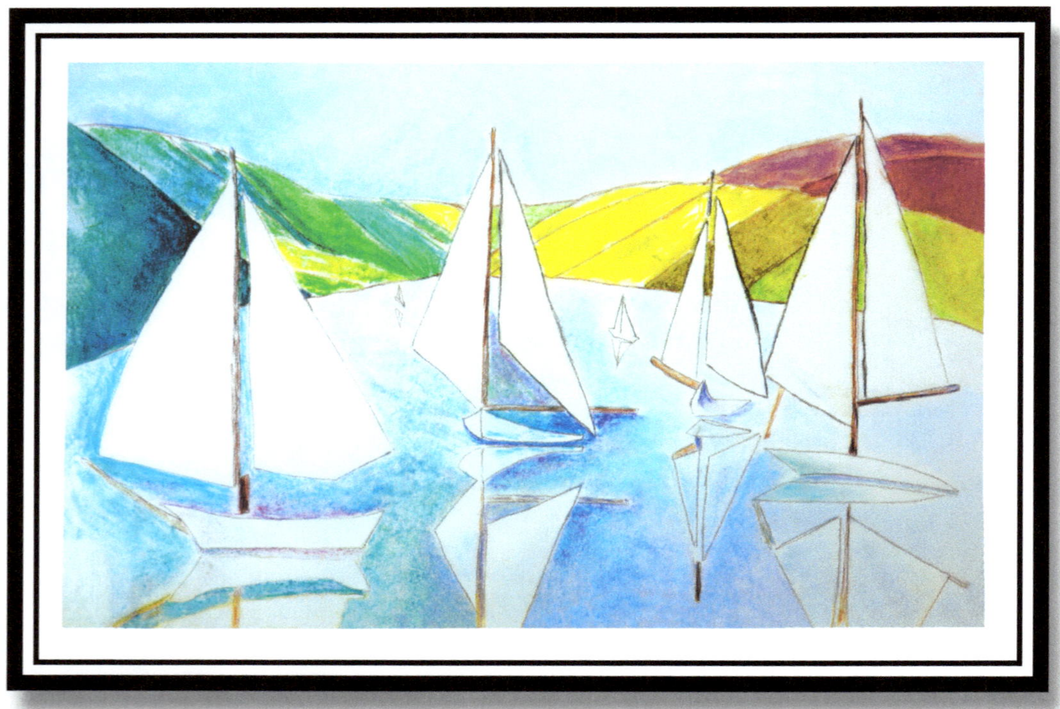

Sailing on
Lake Mascoma

Poems

Part IV

Touches of art

in time

and space.

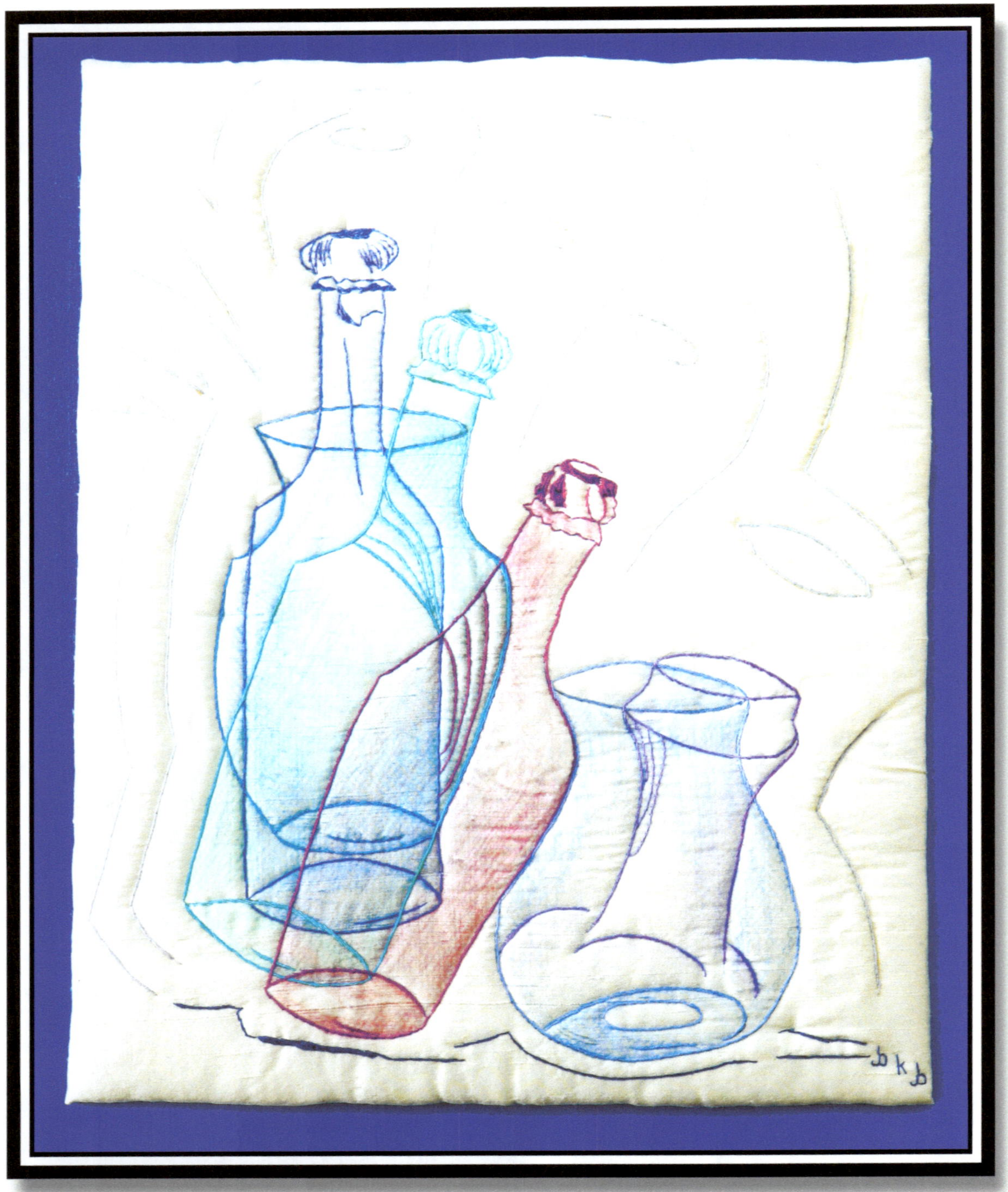

Vases and Bottles in the Abstract

Abstract Art

Abstract art *depends*
not on the laws of shadow or perspective
of natural light and sight.

Abstract art *arises*
from the illusory, the inventive vision
of shape, line, and form.

Abstract art *explores*
new possibilities, the instant impression
of fleeting shapes and shadows, and momentary reflections.

Abstract art *enables*
contours, forms, and their enticing interspaces
to evolve in the mind and escape recessed places.

Abstract art *allows*
use of materials beyond tradition,
to experiment and develop one's individualized expression.

2006

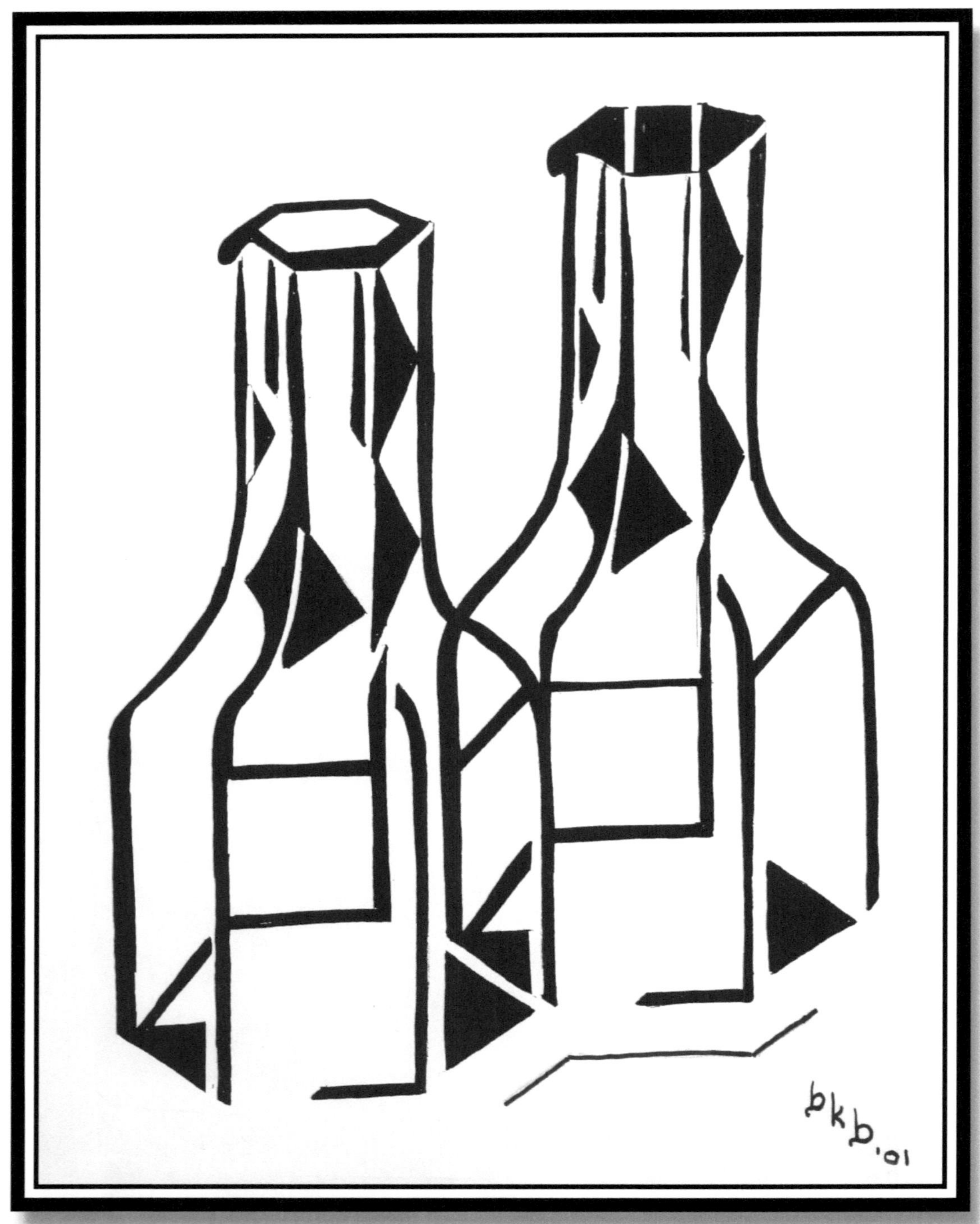

Two Decanters in the Abstract

Touches of Art in Time and Space

My favorite high school subject was geometry,
immediate eye-opener to artistic asymmetry.
This generated a most exciting direction
for me to view objects in the abstract dimension.

When angles, curving lines, and forms
are juxtaposed, their contours are transformed.
I am drawn to the shapes of intervening places
between objects, referred to as "negative spaces."

Pieces of my Scandinavian glass collection,
when arranged by chance or by intention,
create new configurations between the vases
that my love of abstract form richly embraces.

Glass vases play games in early morning light.
Distorted shapes and shadows soon take flight.
Because the sun's patterns last such a brief time,
I record resonating lines in the storehouse of my mind.

I could wait no longer to give these ideas expression.
Returning to school, to study linear impressions,
I was drawn to the history of abstract art.
The Russian avant-garde captured my heart.

2006

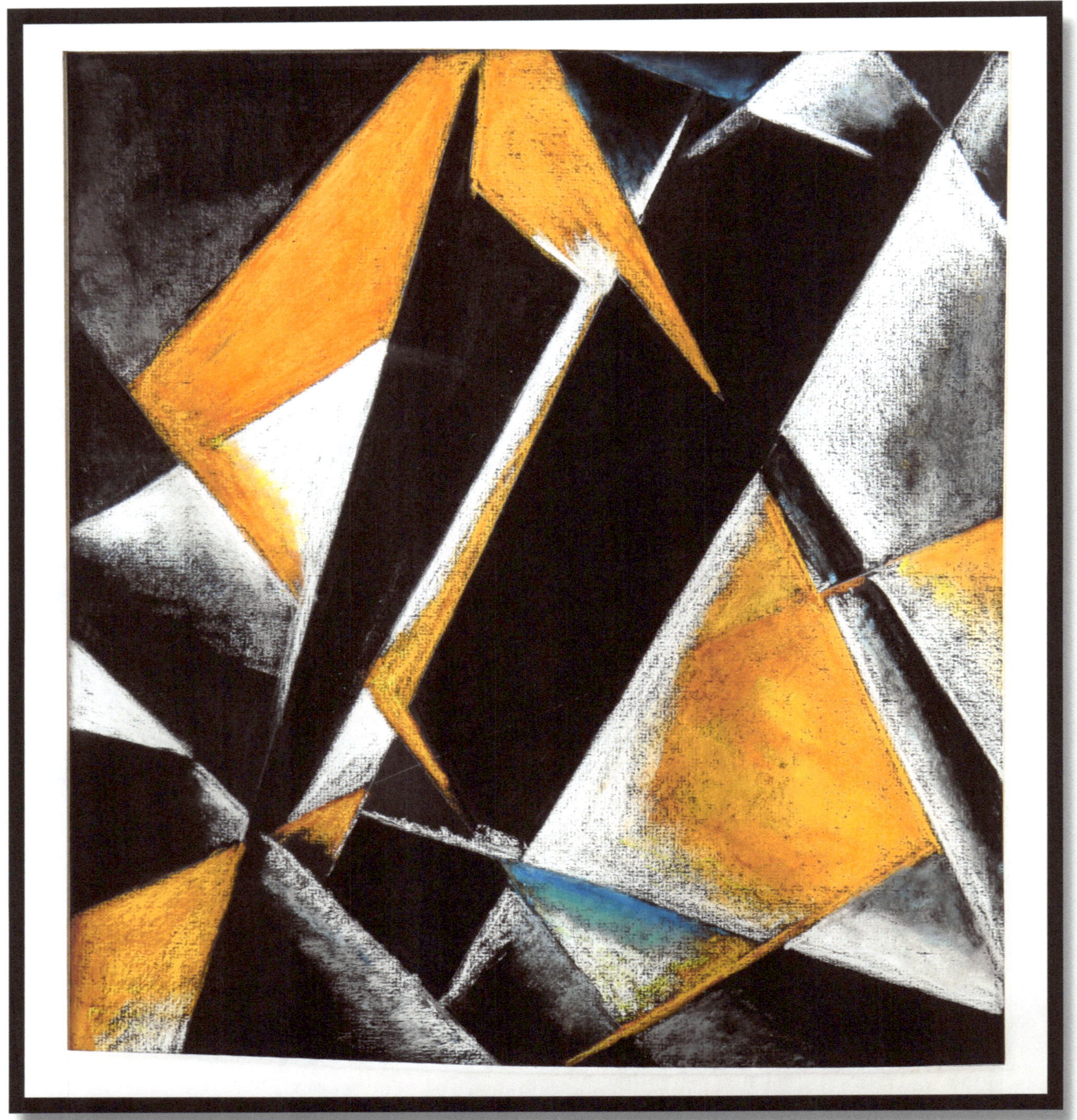

My rendition of Liubov Popova's *Painterly Architectonics*

Popova's Impact

I was drawn to the work of Liubov Popova, so talented, so productive,
so short-lived in Russia. From a photo, I reproduced the shape, line,
and color. It was for me a "tour de force" that I would see much later
on its world tour, of course.

In the Museum of Art in Phoenix, Arizona, at the exhibit of The Painting
Revolution I saw her dramatic original. I was awed by those interlocked
wedges, the subtle colors, and tonal quality at the edges. I recognized
how I could artfully employ, and fully enjoy, the range of her striking innovations.

2006

Tatlin's *Nude*

In St. Petersburg I saw a spectacular exhibit
of formerly hidden, forbidden avant-garde art.

In Moscow I returned to see
Tatlin's famed painting, the *Nude*.

I stood there, still and enchanted.
Tears rolled down my cheeks

as I studied those graceful, curved lines,
lines I had admired and dutifully reproduced.

2006

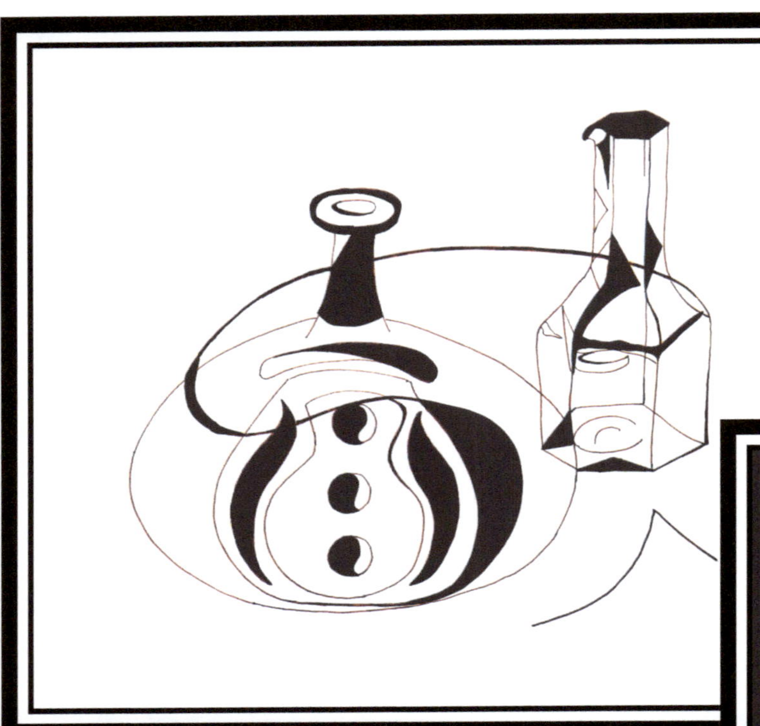

Vase and Decanter

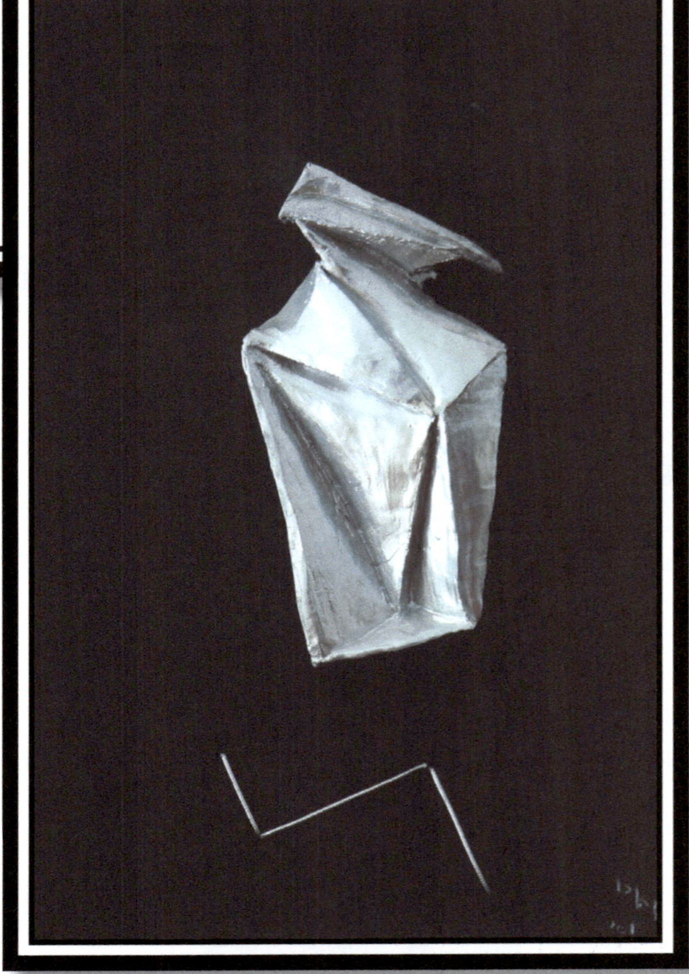

Abstract Pitcher

Demise of Russian Avant-garde Art

The 16th century trade route to Archangel for furs
 became the 20th century gulag site of fury and fears.
From Leningrad's dungeon cells[1] to the frozen seacoast,
 the White Sea Island fortress was what prisoners feared most.
Passing silent church bells in frigid boxcars
 they were soon beyond any emotional scars.
Never could they escape the darkness of winter
 nor the 24-hour brilliance of a northern summer.

The avant-garde artists wanted change,
 change from the rigid czarist's regimes,
change from out-dated art training techniques
 to their new, exciting, unconventional means.[2]

Under Lenin, revolutionary change was what
 these artists applauded and exhorted.
Under Stalin it became a ghastly game
 when lives of many soon were extorted.
The ideas, the concepts, and schools
 of avant-garde artists were then condemned.
More than their lives, existence of the whole
 movement was obliterated in the end.

2006

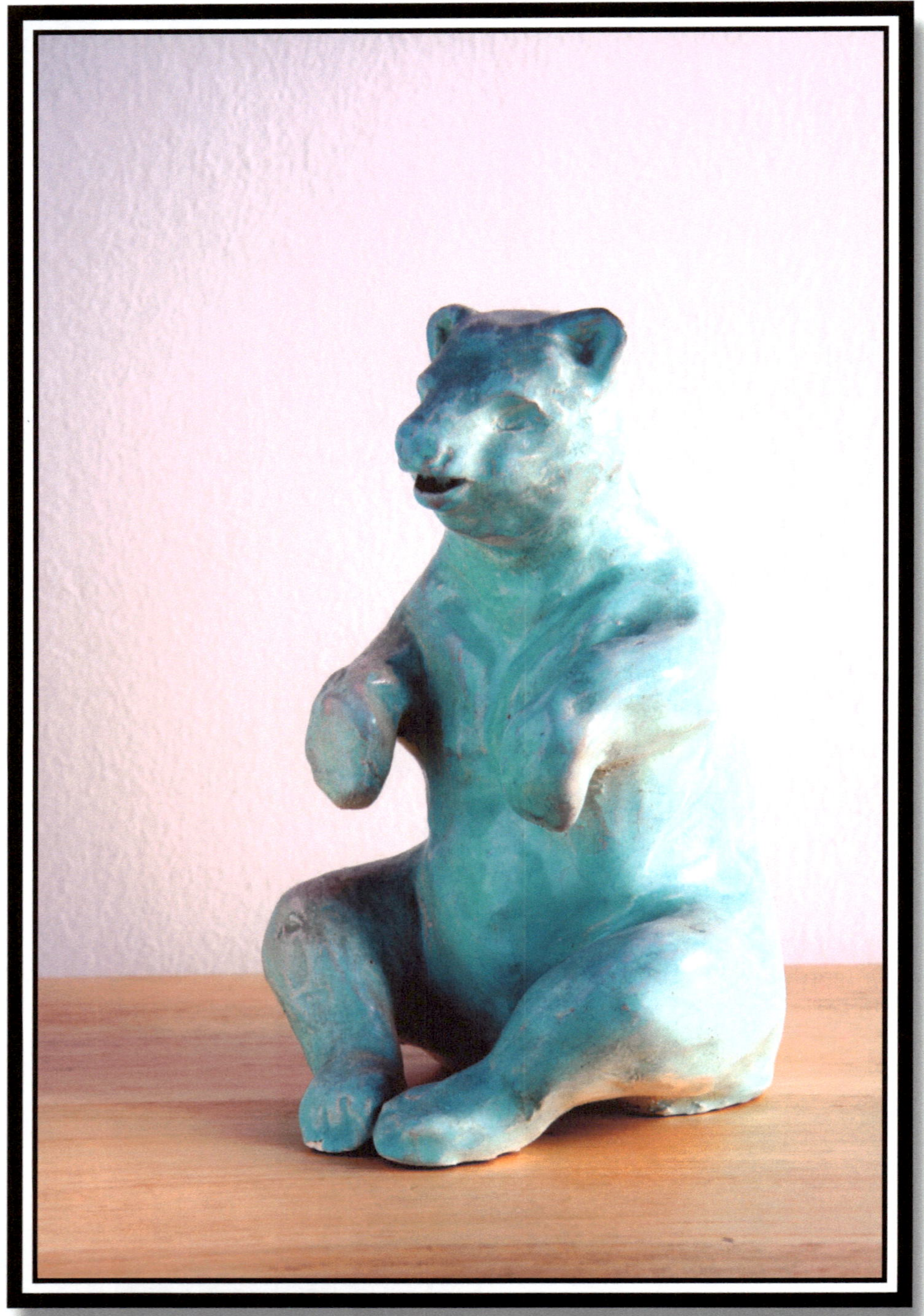

Bear

In Amazement and Gratitude

I am amazed
to learn about those
illiterate peasants
far out in the hinterlands
who risked their lives
to preserve the legacy
of the Russian avant-garde art.

They were commanded
to remove from each museum
any evidence of this
innovative expression.

Those daring, smart people
discovered a remarkable form
of innovative protection.
They built clandestine walls
to hide in blind security,
hundreds of pieces of art,
and preserve them for posterity.

Only after glasnost,
could these brave souls
disclose their secret
and bring it to light.
They unveiled this art
after Gorbachev's thaw,
for the world to witness,
admire and hold in awe.[1]

I am grateful to
those caring peasants
who protected the art
that has become a focus
of deep enrichment
and charmed my heart.

2006

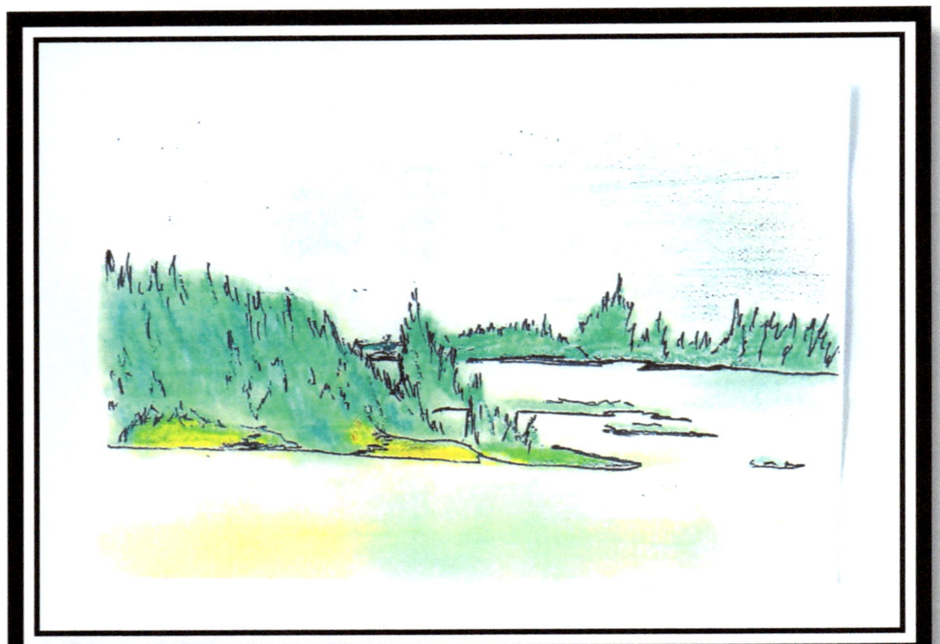

Landscape on the Volga

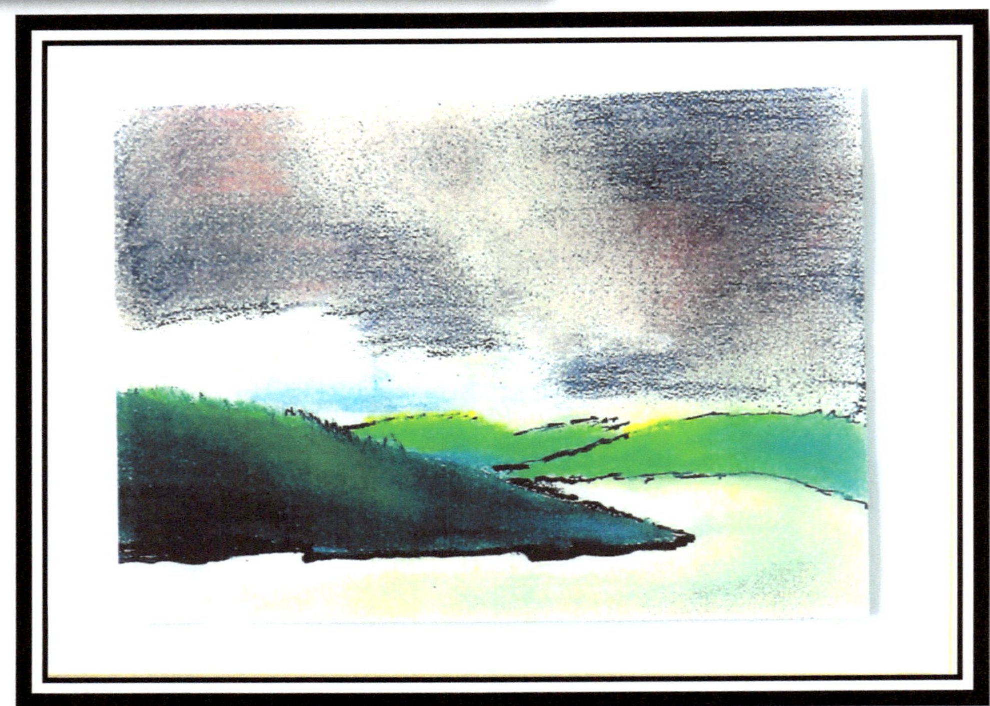

August Skies Bode Winter's Approach

What If?

What if history had passed over
Gorbachev and glasnost?
None of this art would have come to light
—hidden where few knew of its preservation
—forbidden over a bleak sixty-five year duration.
Without glasnost, those courageous souls
could have passed on, forever caring, but never daring
to divulge a revelation, so remarkable, so glaring.

2006

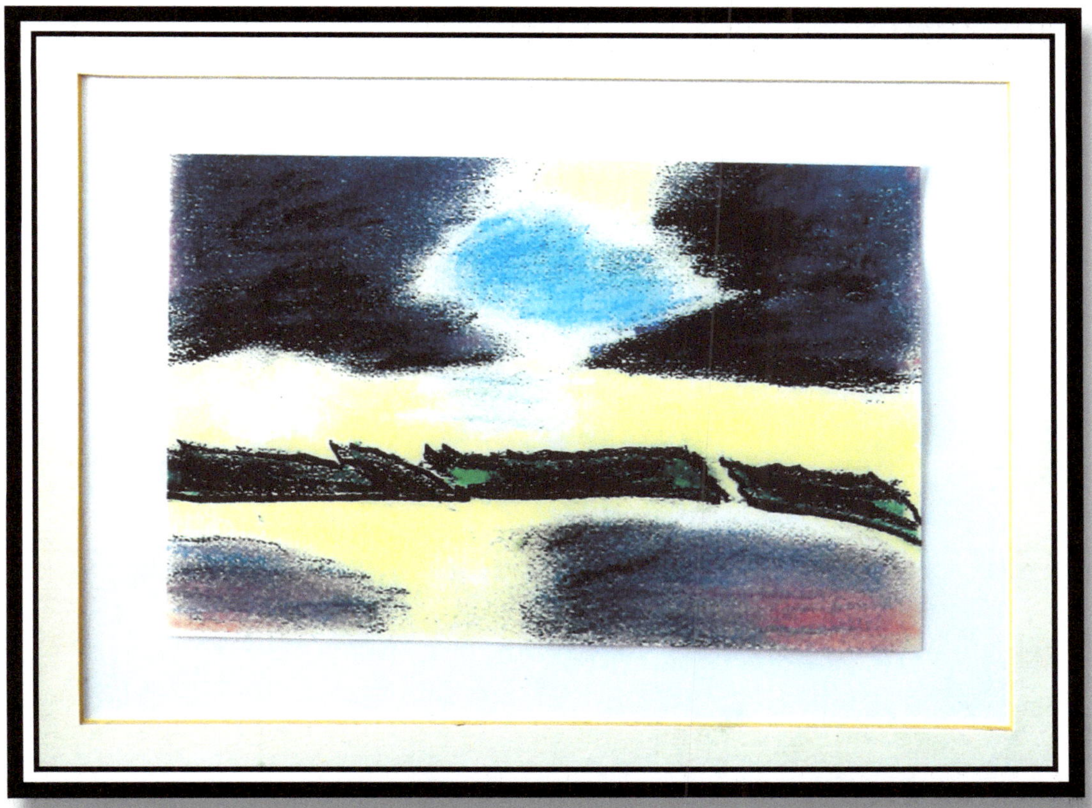

Ominous Skies Open, Like Glasnost

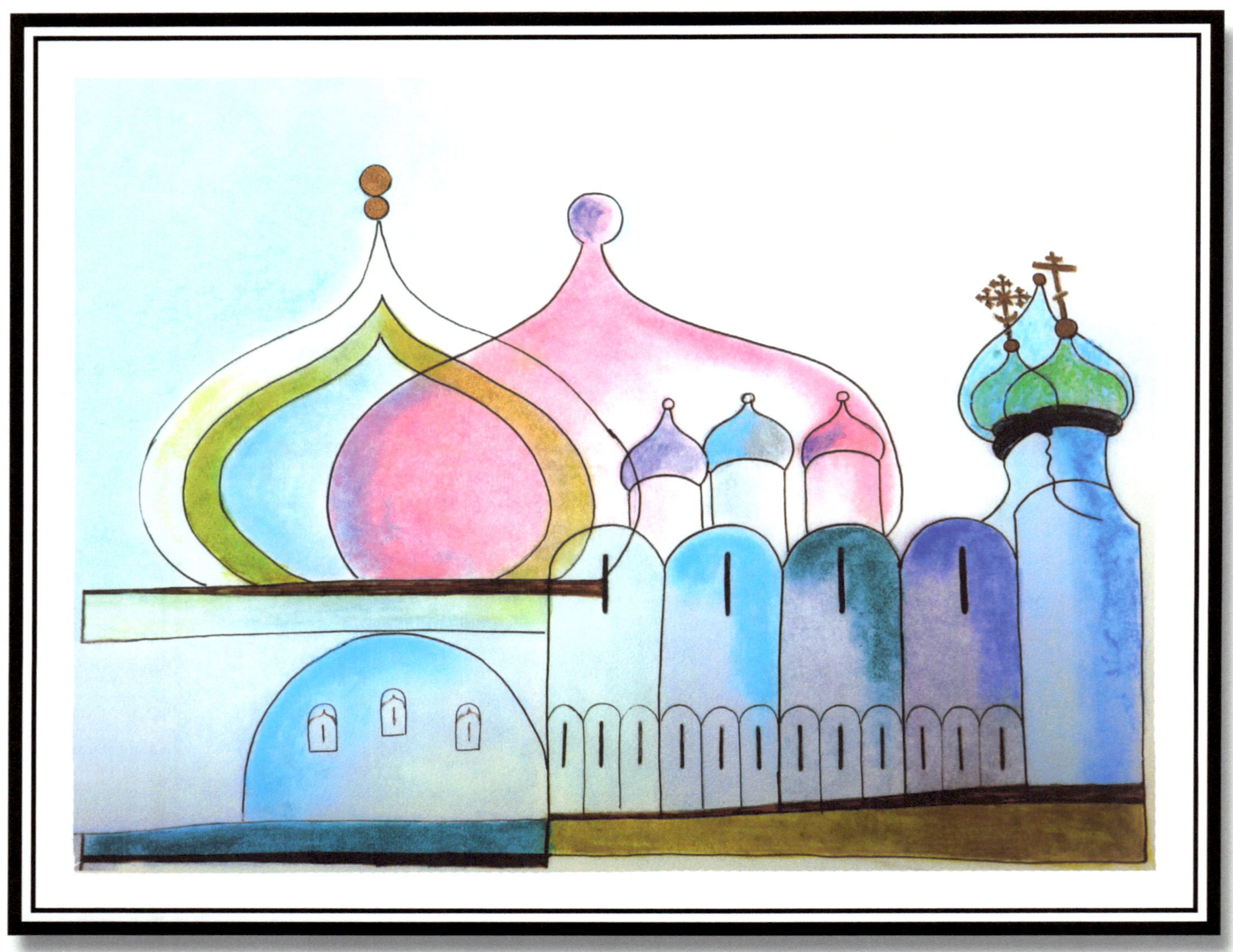

Churches of the Kremlin

The Russian Avant-garde: Past, Present, and Future

In St. Petersburg, good fortune awaited me, surprises too!
I happened upon a "window of opportunity" in 2002.
The State Russian Museum exhibited their avant-garde art,
for just two weeks, which seemed a meager start.

A room full of Kandinskys was poorly attended.
There was little curiosity, few tarried, nor intended
to admire the work of Rodchenko, Filonov,
Natalia Goncharova and her husband Larionov.

Curiously, at this avant-garde exhibit the terse
wall inscription claimed this was their first.
In these fifteen years had their work still been hidden?
Was the exhibit poorly advertised, or its review forbidden?

In Moscow, the famed Tretyiakov Museum had been expanded.
Across from the Kremlin, a mile or so upriver, was erected
the new, modern museum of art, fabricated without flattery.
It has all the grace and architectural charm of an airplane factory.

A remote gallery holds its permanent avant-garde exhibit.
This is a mecca for me. I've been lured back to see it.
Other than tourists, this too, was poorly attended,
but admission might equal their wages, when the day ended.

The question for me arises:
would anyone now be motivated to care
to hide avant-garde art
for future generations to share,
as they did in the hinterland
during Stalin's frightful reign,
in the event the "curtain" drops on Russia
and these creations, again?

2006

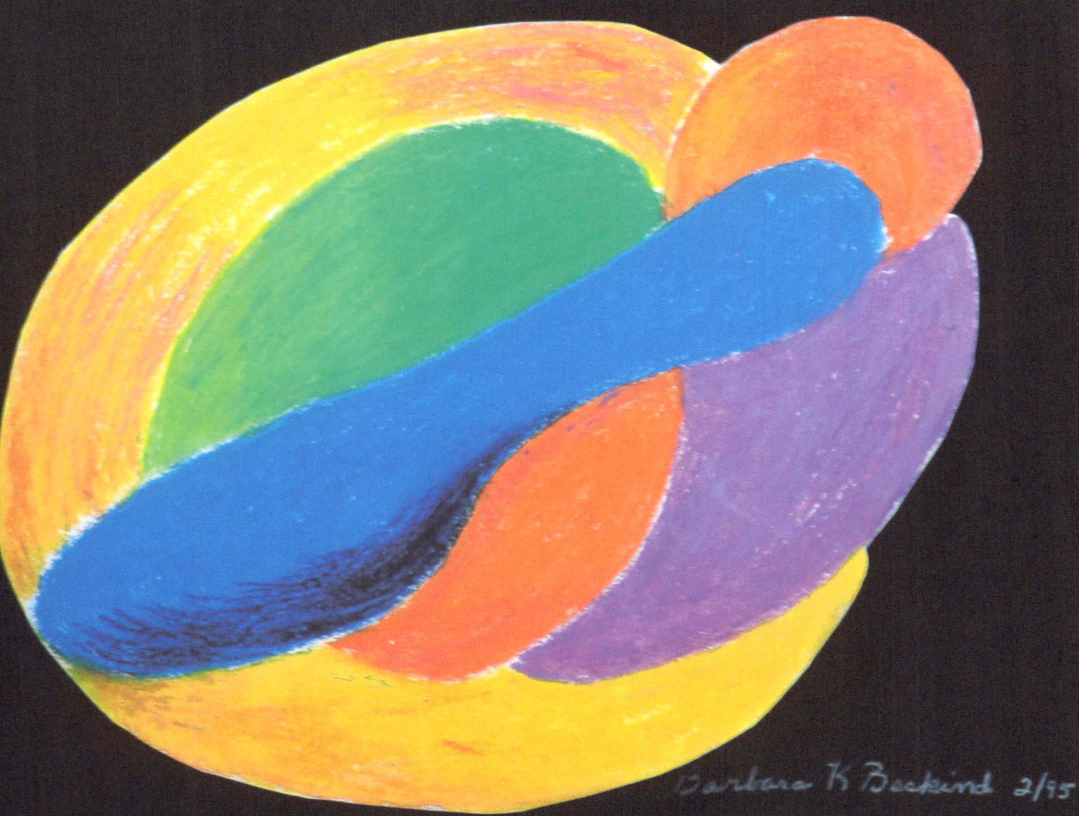

Cinderella’s Shoe

What a Privilege

What a privilege for me to
see those exhibits,[1]
study their artistic explorations,
and integrate their styles,
within my "cut-apart" art, or vivid pastels
that so deeply reflect my regard,
for the remarkable innovations
of the Russian avant-garde.

2006

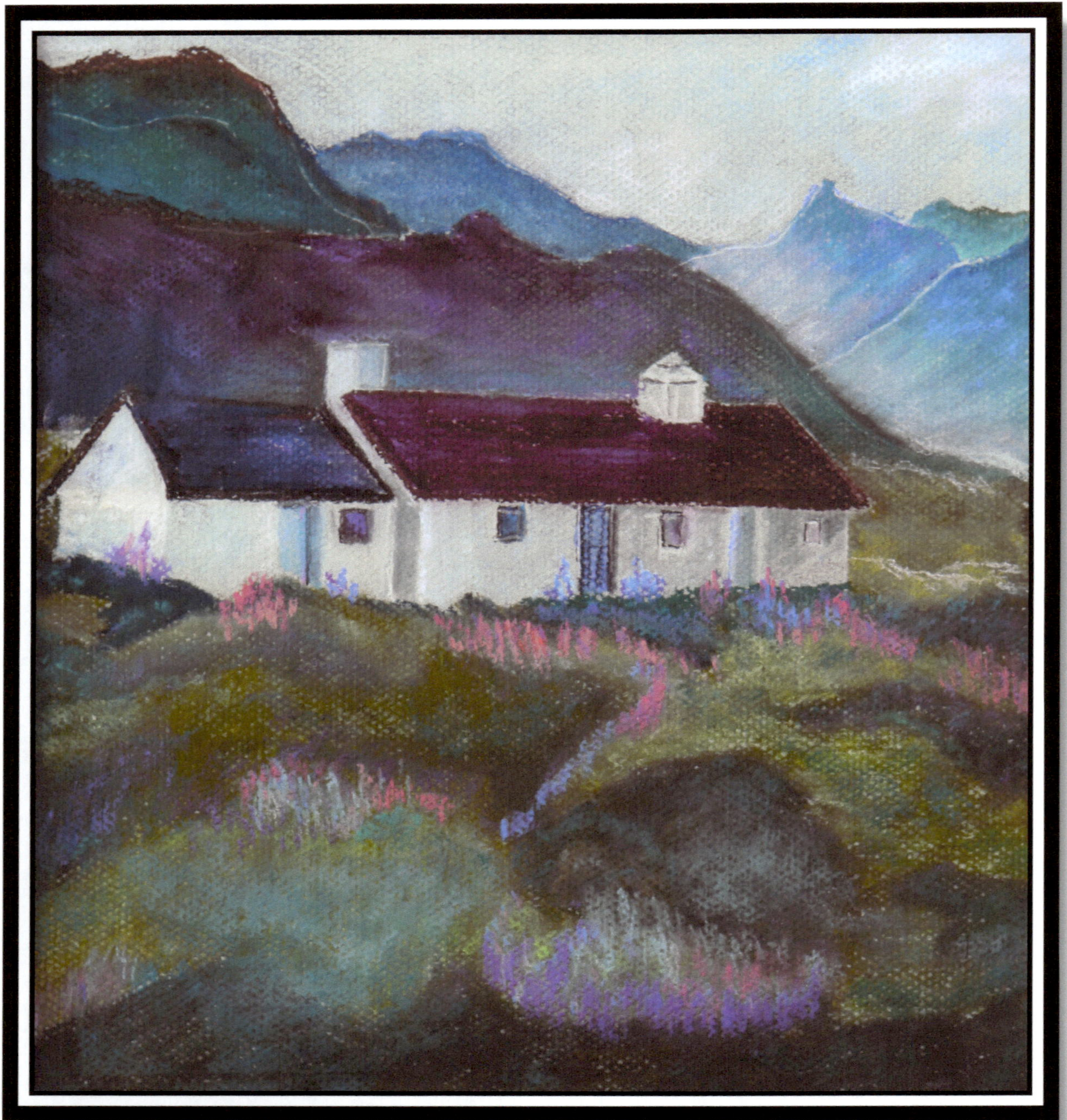

Wildflowers in the Cairngorms

Poems

Part V

Life—that mysterious puzzle

throughout

time and space.

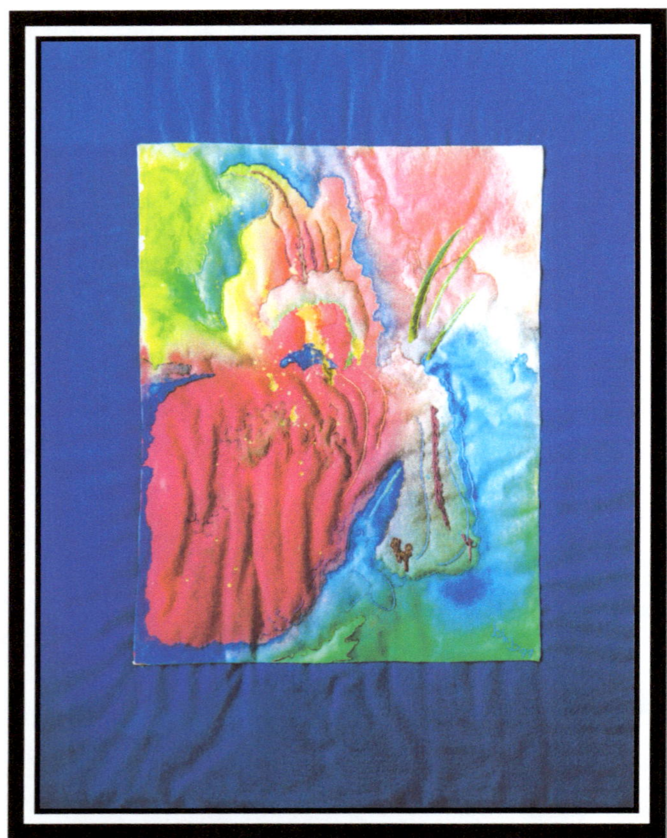

Wild Orchid

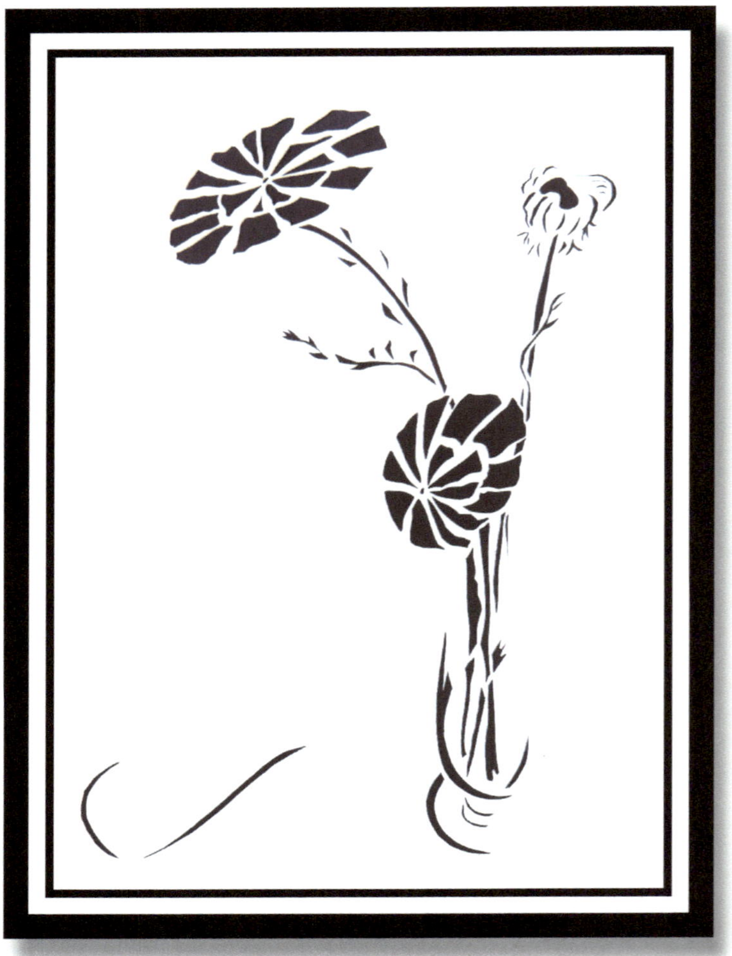

Chrysanthemums

God's Flowerbed

Along country roadsides
weeds and bright wildflowers
bloom across God's flowerbed.

Sky-blue chicory and wild white daisies
grow beside day lilies
and Devil's paint-brush.

Purple loosestrife, goldenrod,
and heather
cover God's garden in fall.

What I enjoy most are the spring woodlands
dotted with trillium and wild orchid
hiding unseen as intruders pass.

Blossoms from God's flowerbed
are a colorful inspiration
for my art.

I express it with pastels, watercolors,
or embroidery thread applied to
Egyptian cotton or Dupioni silk.

And the essence can be captured
without color at all in black and white
"cut-apart" art.

Some interpret this piece of "cut-apart" art
as a chrysanthemum,
others as Queen Anne's lace.

Whichever you see is your call.

2006

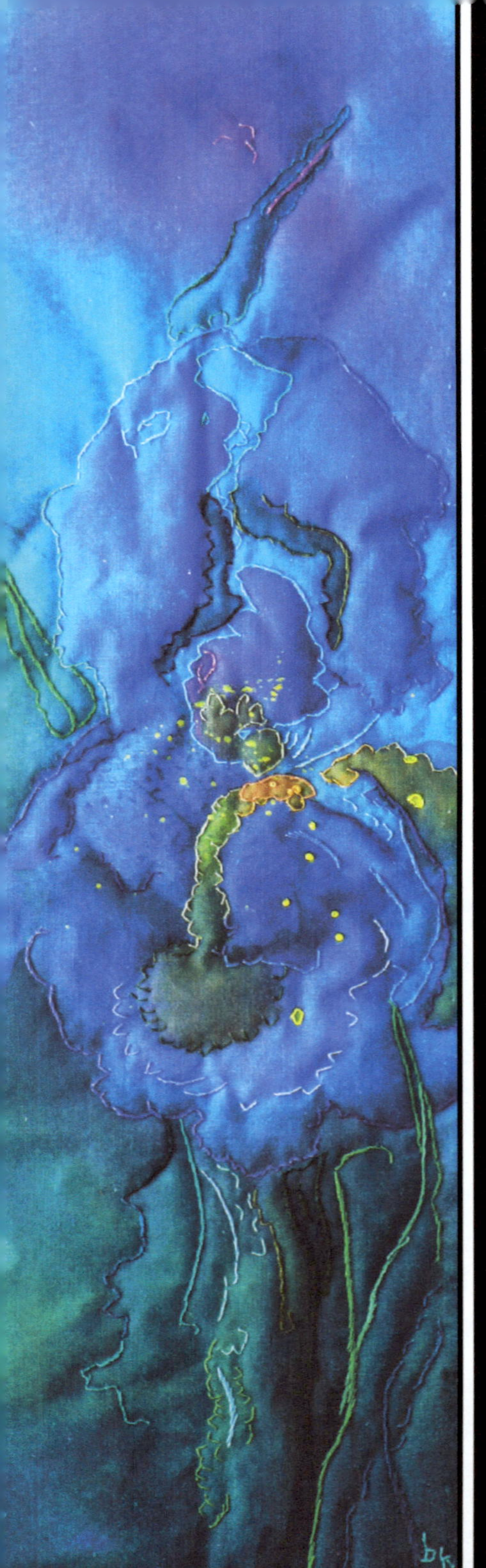

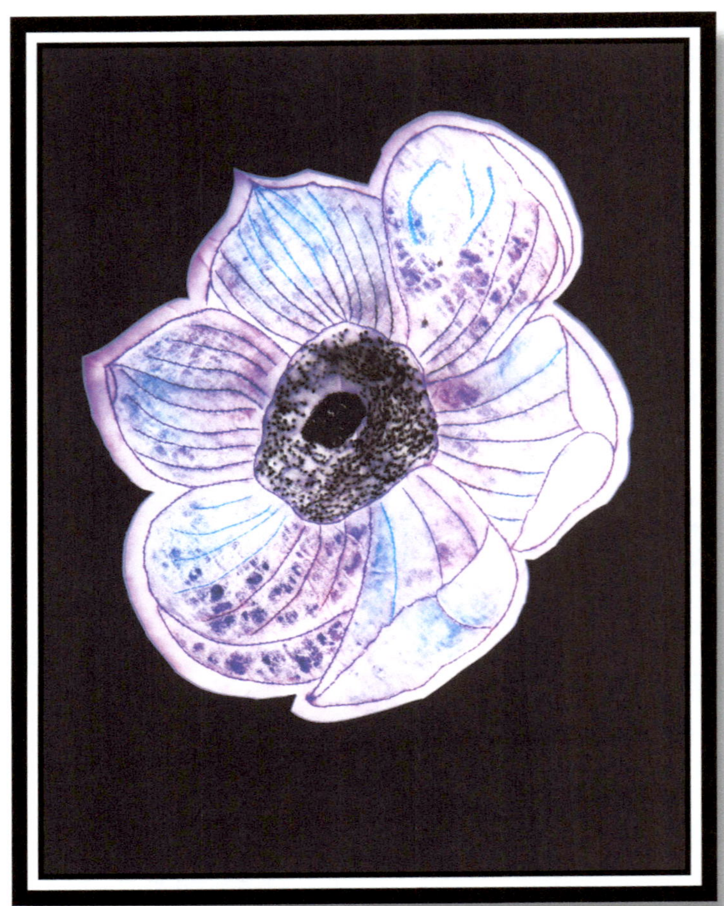

Lavender Anemone

Iris in Blue

With a Needle in My Hand

Artist, and magician with a needle,
my mother laundered and restored
antique textiles that were rent or broken
for a tiny income, to keep our poverty unspoken.

I was at my mother's arm
from the time I could first stand,
watching as she made our clothes,
mended family socks, shirts, and pants.

Then, when I could reach the treadle
and guide fabric beneath the needle,
I would make clothes to cover
my extended family, the dolls.

French knots and cross-stitch
patterns gradually came alive
as my mother embroidered
each evening and I would be close by.

Every gesture, every knot
is embedded in my memory
and as soon as I thread a needle,
that joy of movement is revived.

Thus my art developed into
hand-embroidered wall hangings
on cotton and silk, padded from beneath
to become a softly-sculptured "bas-relief."

2006

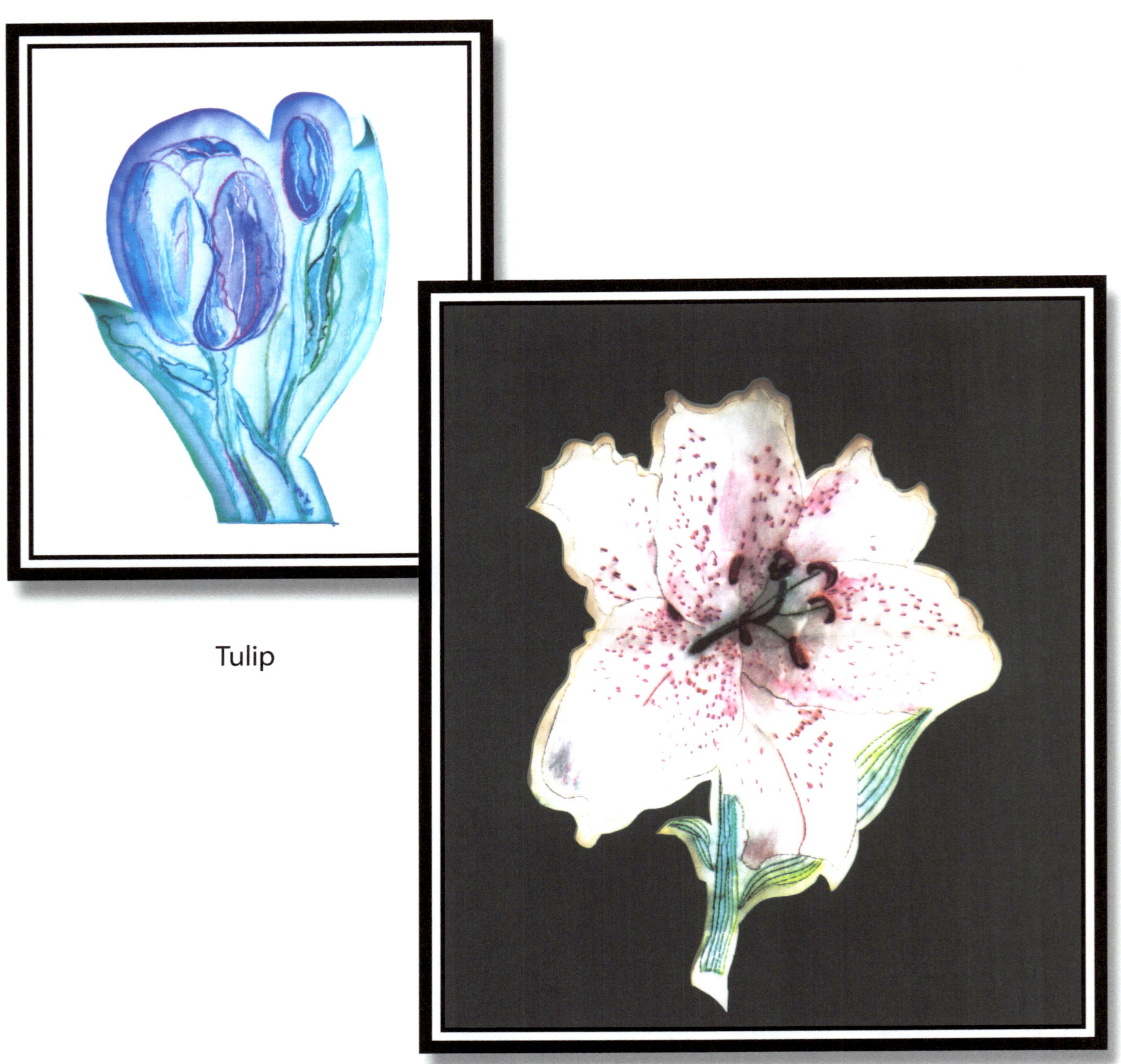

Tulip

Casablanca Lily

My Garden, My Inspiration

Flowers from my garden
are an inspiration for my art.

The height of my success year after year
was to grow thirteen blooms

of a Casablanca lily with white,
textured petals on a single stalk.

I grew it
I drew it
then I painted it on silk,
embroidered and matted it
in a translucent
sculpture-cut mat framed
so the sun could penetrate
it through the windowpane.

The tulips, the iris, the lilies galore,
daisies, bachelor buttons, and poppies, I adore.

My artistic inspiration
draws directly from my legacies:

my grandmother's garden tools,
my mother's embroidery skills.

In my art, these legacies bring two individuals
closer together than they ever were.

As a child I rejected grandma, found
distasteful her poetry of old.

I've come full circle now, to enjoy poetic rhythms,
to express feelings I never dared to share with her soul.

Thus, in a most unpredictable, countervailing manner
gardening, poetry, and the art of embroidery

mysteriously bring the three of us together.

2006

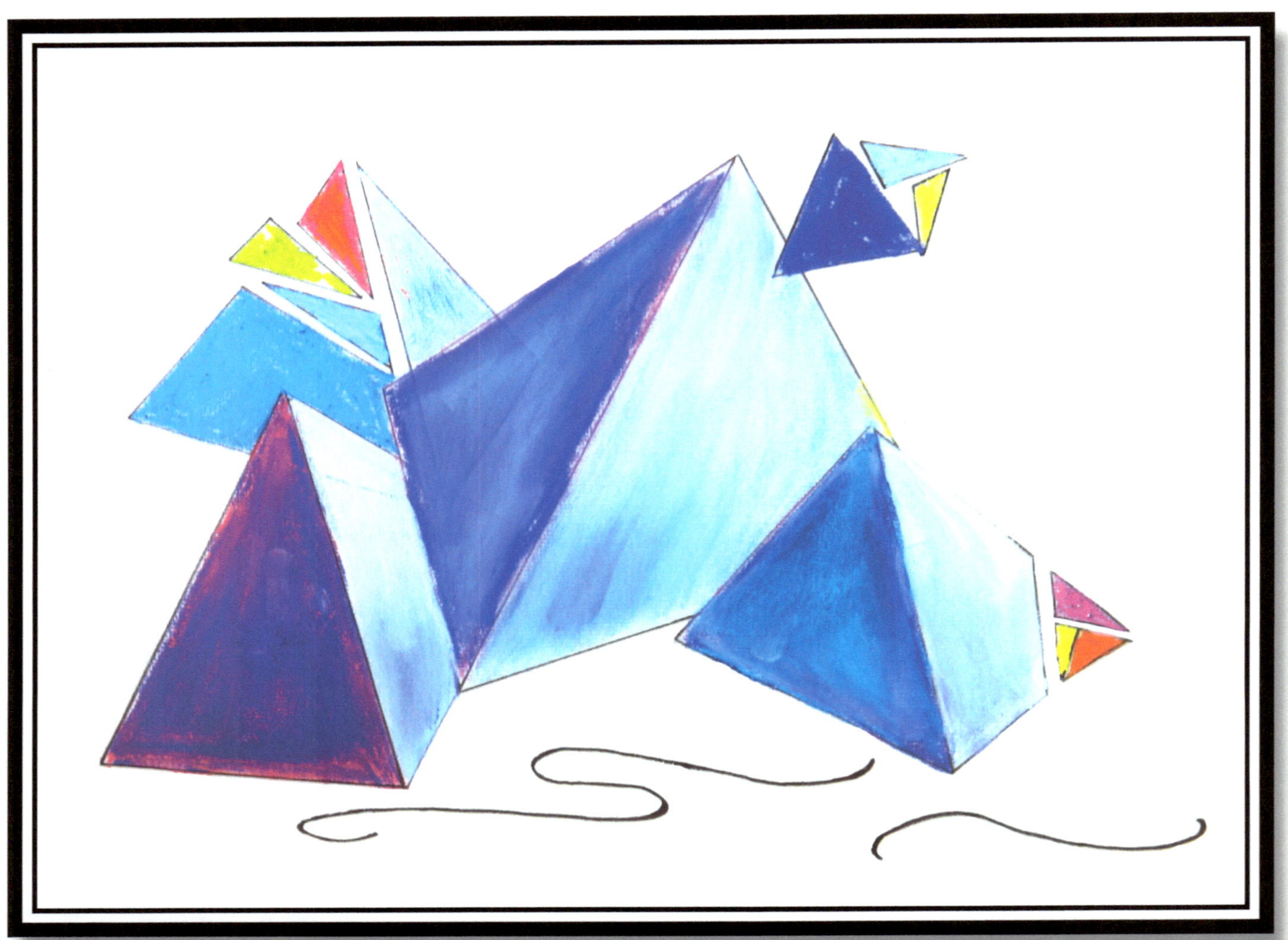

Life's Mysterious Puzzle

Life's Mysterious Puzzle

In these matured years of my life

the most exciting, illuminating, and gratifying aspect

has been to see many disparate parts and struggles

that have seemed unrelated, unproductive at the time

become warm touches of life in time and space.

When I discover the pieces for those places,

I find they fit ever so closely

to complete the unfolding picture

of life's mysterious puzzle.

2006

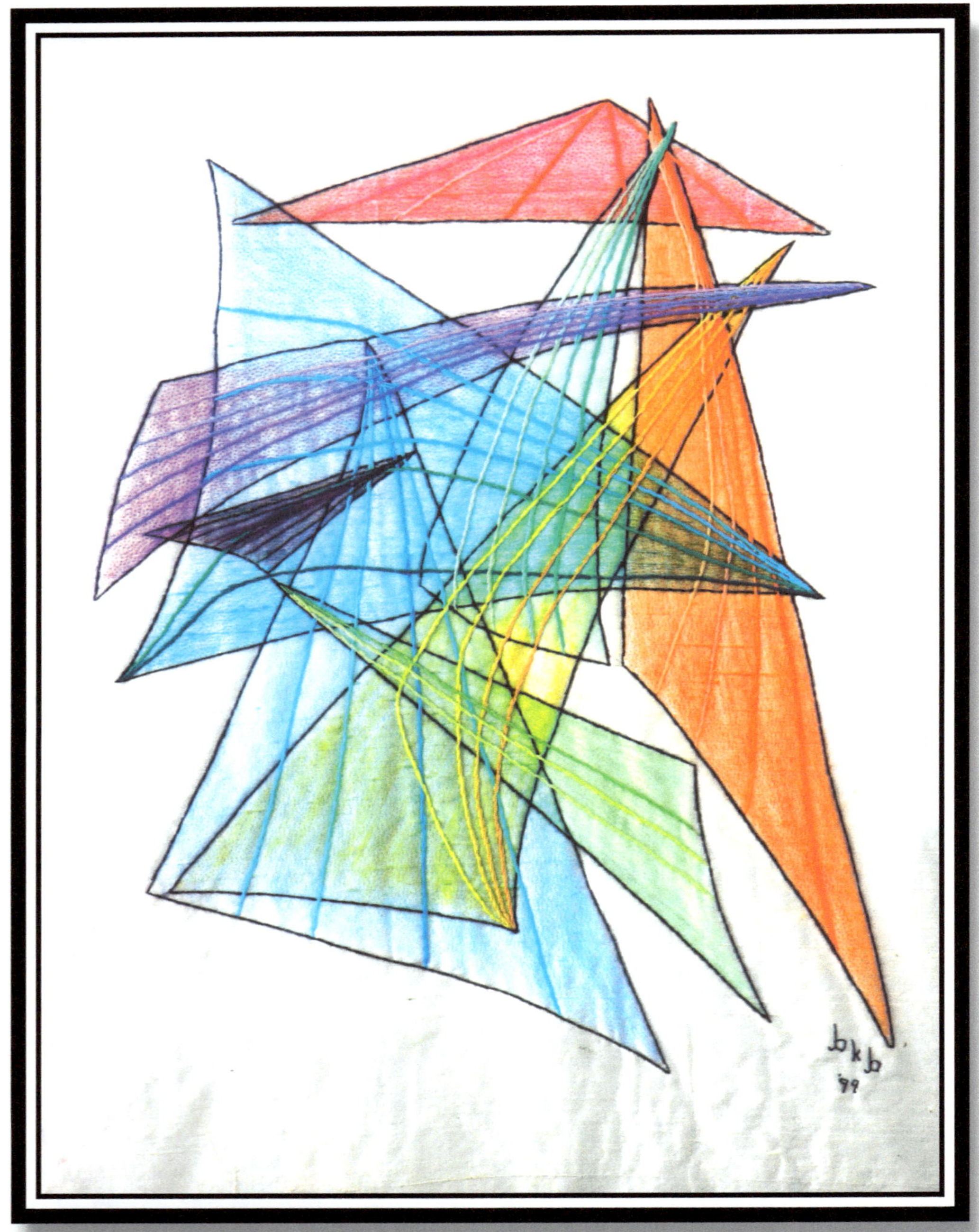

Life's Many Stages and Interactions

Life Itself

Life itself must carry me
across the abyss
to taste the fruits of amazement,
not floundering, not wishful, nor unfulfilled,
but on a journey of enrichment, of humor, of expectation.

Like music that is thrust into silence and dies
my life too will end,
but I want that silence to resonate
with all the eager involvement
about every aspect of life available to me.

I strive to uncover life's secrets
for these are the hidden treasures that open up to us
because we care, we try, we want to participate.

Never do I want to reach the gate
at the end of life's journey
only as an observer.

1996

Footnotes for the Poems

Surprise Aboard Hudson's *Half Moon,* page 19

1 Douglas Corrigan filed a flight plan to head west from Brooklyn's Floyd Bennett Field, but on July 8, 1938, he landed his single engine plane in Ireland instead, earning him the humorous nick-name "wrong-way Corrigan."

2 Hudson's two earlier voyages to find a northeast passage resulted in failure.

3 The Merchant Adventurers had bought the old Muscovy Company (of London), so named because its ships sailed to Archangel on the White Sea, to buy Muscovite furs for the European market of the 1500s. (An island fortress on the White Sea became one of Stalin's gulags for thousands of prisoners.) See poem, page 71.

4 The route to the Orient around the Cape of Good Hope was subject to treacherous tropical storms and worse yet, capture by Spanish and Portuguese pirates.

5 Trondheim is pronounced Tron-yem and sounds like them.

6 The Mohawk River was not navigable due to the 65-foot high Cohoes Falls a few miles west of the Hudson River.

The Other Half Moon, page 23

1 Currently Mechanicville, New York.

2 rhymes with play

3 The French, secret allies of the English in this Anglo-Dutch War, quickly invaded the Low Countries under the direction of Louis XIV of France. (See Bradley in the Bibliography.) Harmon's home Province of North Brabant had been over-run by the French forces, circa 1672.

4 1674

5 The location originally carrying this name is now called Mechanicville, N.Y. The town currently carrying the name of Half Moon lies a few miles to the southwest. Across the Hudson from the original Half Moon and three miles to the east, lies the Knickerbocker Mansion, at Schaghticoke, New York. It is on the National Historic Registry.

6 History of Hudson's ship having reached as far up the river as the point where Albany now stands is substantiated in *Charting the Sea of Darkness* by Donald S. Johnson, 1993. (See Bibliography.)

The Miles Standish Cocktail Party, page 27

1 The spelling of Myles had been changed to Miles by this time.

2 Representing the Poughkeepsie District of Dutchess County, New York.

Ode to Conradt Ham, page 31

1 I was stationed at the 98th Army General Hospital along the banks of the Nahe River at Neubrûcke (1955–1957) as an occupational therapist and Captain in the Army Medical Specialist Corps.

2 The Second Spanish Inquisition was conducted under the Duke of Alva between 1567 and 1579 in the Walloon Provinces of the Belgic Lands that became part of Belgium in 1830.

3 It would appear that Conradt Ham's family originally had been Walloons who fled Hainaut Province of the Belgic Lands.

My Walloon Ancestors. page 33

1 They were early followers of John Calvin. See Addendum A.

2 Pronounced Tour-nye, rhymes with high.

3 Original spelling. See Addendum D.

4 Details of this period appear in *Powder Keg*, Part II, Chapter 3.

5 The Conradt Hams' family line.

Ancestors of Choice, page 35

1 The term can mean distant relative, especially one through marriage; in some regions it refers to children conceived, or born, out of wedlock, often to be disclaimed.

2 The name is also spelled Germond, German, or Jarmin. See Addendum E.

3 Roman Catholics of that era were called Papists.

Letter to Grandma "K" pg 41

1 Grandma Knickerbocker

Demise of Russian Avant-garde Art, page 71

1 These dungeons were located within the Peter and Paul Fortress, an island on the Neva River in St. Petersburg. The name of this city was changed to Petrograd in 1914, was renamed Leningrad in 1924, then reverted to St. Petersburg in 1991.

2 See Addendum G.

In Amazement and Gratitude, pg 73

1 1987

What a Privilege, page 79

1 *The Painterly Revolution: Kandinsky, Malevich and the Avant-garde* at the Museum of Art, Phoenix, Arizona (2000), *Art of the Avant-garde Exhibit* at the State Russian Museum, St Petersburg (2002), *The Avant-garde Exhibit* at the State Museum-Exhibition Center (ROSIZO) (The New Tretyiakov Museum), Moscow, (2002), *The Avant-garde Exhibit*, at the Guggenheim Museum, New York City, New York (2002), *The Russian Avant-garde Exhibit*, at the Walters Art Gallery, Baltimore, MD, (2003) and *The Avant-garde Exhibit* at the State Museum–Exhibit Center (ROSIZO), (The New Tretyiakov Museum) Moscow, (2003).

Addendum A: The Walloons

The Walloons referred to here were Calvinist followers who lived in the Walloon Provinces of the Belgic Lands north of France in the early, formative years of the Protestant Reformation. Other Walloons living there at that time, and now, remained Catholic.

Followers of Calvin in France were called Huguenots; in the Belgic Lands, which became Belgium in 1830, they were referred to as Walloon Reformists. In The Netherlands they were, and are, Dutch Reformed, and in Scotland they are Presbyterians.

Addendum B: Admiral de Ruyter and the 1672 Battle of Solebay

Admiral Michiel Adriaan de Ruyter, the most famous admiral in Dutch history, led the opening salvo of the 3rd Anglo-Dutch War with 70 ships in the Battle of Solebay on June 7, 1672. (Authorities differ as to the date; others report May 28, 1672.) The English and French fleets were at anchor off Solebay on the eastern coast of England to be refitted in preparation for a blockade of Dutch ports.

Admiral de Ruyter's strategy to send out two ships under the full moon to scout the location of the English and French fleets is lauded in the annals of naval history of the time.

This surprise attack at dawn sent the French fleet heading out to the English Channel, and several British and Dutch ships to the bottom. Although the result was a draw, the Dutch action had successfully prevented a blockade of their ports and Dutch access to the North Sea. (See bibliography for David Marley.)

Addendum C: Washington Irving and the "Knickerbocker" name

The original spelling of the family name was changed permanently after 1809 when Washington Irving first published his parody, *The Knickerbocker History of New York by Diedrich Knickerbocker.*

Washington Irving was a personal friend of Harman Knickerbakker, who was a U.S. Congressman from the 11th District for New York State and who owned the Mansion at Schaghticoke, New York. Washington Irving took his "nom de plume" from the 15-year-old nephew Dietrich, who lived next door. It is said that parts of the book were written in the front room of the Mansion during his stays there.

Addendum D: Nieuw Amsterdam

The name, originally spelled Nieuw Amsterdam by the Dutch, was changed to New York when Richard Nicolls arrived to take over the city for the British on September 8th, 1664.

On August 9, 1673, the Dutch reclaimed it. For the next 13 months it was named Nieuw Orange. The British resumed claim through the Treaty of Westminster in 1674, and the name New York has remained.

Addendum E: Lineage of Charles Germaine

Relevant lineage of Charles Germaine, also spelled Germond, German, and Jarmin.

He had six children:

Margaret, married Paix Cassaneau after 1691
Mary, married Andre Sigourney 2nd
Charles Jr.
Ober
Peter
Isaac German moved to Dutchess County on, or before, 1736 and married. He died in 1763. His children were:

Isaac Jr. who married in 1736 to Catherine Haff.
Susanne, married in 1736 to Lawrence Haff.
James died, 1788.
Peter baptized November 6th, 1760.[1]
Seaman " November 6th, 1760.
Phebe " November 6th, 1760.
Deborah " November 6th, 1760.
Sarah " November 6th, 1760, married Jonathan Vincent.[2]

Sarah Germond,[3] was born July 10th, 1760 and died November 22nd, 1795 at the age of 35. She married Jonathan Vincent on October 1st, 1780.

They had 6 children; the 6th was Gilbert Issac, who had 13 children and the 5th of that generation was Jonathan Vincent. He was the grandfather of Mary Vincent who married Jonathan Ham.

They had 5 children, the oldest of whom was my grandfather, Eugene Ham. Their oldest child of 6 was my mother, Mary Ham.

I am the end of this line, the 10th documented generation of the Huguenot fugitive of La Tremblade Prison, Charles Germaine, who fled in 1687.[4]

---

1 It was common practice then to have the children of various ages all baptized at one time, when the traveling pastor was available.

2 See *The Vincent Family, Descendants of Adrian Vincent*, Millbrook Press, Millbrook, New York 1959.

3 Great grand-daughter of Charles Germaine.

4 February 21, 1976 I married Harry Beskind, MD in Princeton, New Jersey. I have two step-sons, Mark and Daniel. On June 16, 1994, my husband and I were divorced.

Addendum F: Details with regard to the Star of David

First, the hand-embroidered Star of David is included here in memory of my late mother-in-law, Sadie (Teitlebaum) Beskind.

Second, the Star of David is included here because of my fascination in finding parallels between the Diaspora of the Jews from Spain after the Spanish Inquisition in 1492, with that of the Walloon Reformists from their Belgic homeland 75 years later during the virtually unknown Second Spanish Inquisition.

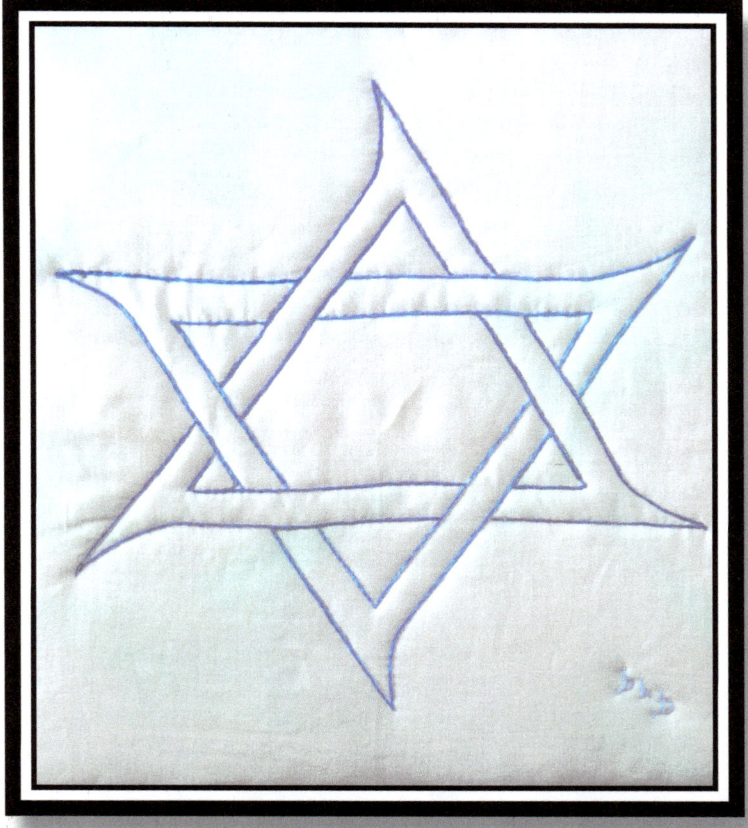

Third, the Jews, and the Walloon Reformists who were the first settlers to arrive in early Nieuw Amsterdam, shared an unexpected, little-known piece of history. The first Dutch Reformed Church services in North America (1628) and services of the first Jewish congregation in North America, the Shearith Israel Congregation, (circa 1656) each transpired on the second floor of Francois Molemacher's horse-driven grist mill at 22 Slyck Steeg, re-named by the British as Mill Street, now called South William Street, in lower Manhattan.[1]

History reveals that the first Jewish Synagogue built in North America, the Mill Street Synagogue, and called "The Little Synagogue" (35' x 35'), was erected in 1730 on this site.[2] This Spanish and Portuguese Congregation of Shearith Israel moved three more times. The current Shearith Israel Synagogue is located at 70th Street and Central Park West, in New York City.[3] Traditionally, services of these Sephardic Jews[4] were held in Portuguese.[5]

1 It is presumed that my early ancestor Walloon Adrian Vincent, who arrived in 1634, and who lived around the block on the Herre Gracht, now Broad Street, and owned the tavern on the corner of Slyck Steeg and the Herre Gracht, had attended the Dutch Reformed services held at Molemacher's grist mill, the only available space. Although the Dutch Reformed Church in Holland supplied the pastor, services apparently were conducted in the Walloon dialect of French.

2 Detailed history of this is presented in Part II, Chapter 2 of *Powder Keg* by Barbara Knickerbocker, published by BKB Press, New London, NH 2008.

3 Whereas the Mill Street Synagogue was the first ever built in North America (1730), and its congregation, Shearith Israel is the oldest (1654), Truro Synagogue in Newport, Rhode Island, is the oldest standing Synagogue in this hemisphere, dedicated in 1763.

4 Jews whose families originated in Spain. Many emigrated to Portugal and were expelled three years later, in 1495.

5 This history is presented in Part II, Chapter 2 of *Powder Keg* by Barbara Knickerbocker, published by BKB Press, New London, NH, 2008.

Addendum G: Art of the Russian Avant-garde[1] (1910–1922)

In order to present the complexities of the Russian avant-garde, and the reasons for its mercurial rise and fall, it is vital to cite brief references to the art of Czarist Russia, and that which came earlier. For instance, it may be surprising to find that the roots of abstract art of the Russian avant-garde originated in the time-honored Russian Orthodox church schools of icon painting of the 12th to 15th centuries.

The Russian avant-garde art movement began in 1910 and flourished rapidly over the next twelve years. Various innovative styles of abstract art, sculpture, and architecture included: Cubo-Futurism (Kluin), Neo-Primitivism (Larionov), Suprematism (Malevich),[2] and Constructivism (Rodchenko, Gabo, Tatlin, El Lizitsky).

One reason for the fluidity and swift expansion of the avant-garde movement was the fact there were no patriarchs to advocate an individual style. Participants were young people, many of whom had come from families of wealth who sent them abroad to study art. At the outbreak of World War I, all Russians were called back to their motherland. These young students returned, excited by the works of Cezanne, Picasso, Matisse, and Brancusi as well as the Italian Futurists. During the war and after, news of any kind, to include the development of the avant-garde, was curtailed. This was further restricted after Stalin came to power. Since it symbolized freedom of expression, the avant-garde was an embarrassment to the Communists to be obliterated throughout the Soviet Union.

This innovative Russian avant-garde movement may be characterized best by its rugged individualism. It arose out of a geographically broad, culturally-diverse range of artists. They came from Armenia, Georgia, the Ukraine, the Black Sea and Baltic Sea coasts, and included those of culturally-rich Jewish and Polish origins. Although they spoke a number of languages, the language of art was easily communicated among them. Artists best known in the west are Vasilii Kandinsky, Naum Gabo, and Marc Chagall.

The Russian avant-garde comprised not only artists in the visual arts. It was a highly integrated community encompassing art, sculpture, architecture, literature, and theatre. Since none of the museums of Czarist Russia would accept their work, set design and theatrical costuming became the principal early, public showcase of the avant-garde.[3]

In addition to there being no patriarchal figure, there were many other reasons why no single individual, or identifiable "style" defines this free-wheeling "avant-garde."

Artists were incredibly competitive. Many presented well-reasoned theoretical treatises about their work in art publications and the lay press.

The single, unifying force of the avant-garde was their aversion to the traditional studio training so highly regarded at the Academy of Art of St. Petersburg, the prestigious art center of Czarist Russia. The avant-garde considered it anathema to use plaster models rather than live ones. They also rejected the regimented training in representational realism.

The uncharted, rapid expansion of their innovative ideas and non-traditional use of materials soon led these young artists to agitate for greater personal freedoms. Many believed it was their mandate to enlighten the masses about the freedoms they were beginning to espouse as individuals.

Therefore, rumblings of the Bolsheviks to advance radical change met sympathetic ears well before the Revolution. The 1917 October Revolution advocated the destruction of the old cultural and political order. This enabled the radical nature of the avant-garde to thrive.

---

1 This is a point of view I have evolved over the past decade through comprehensive study, observations of exhibitions in this country and in Russia, and traveling the terrain native to some of these artists. I have drawn heavily on the following to establish my own interpretations: the exhibition catalog of the *Painting Revolution: Kandinsky, Malevich and Others*, the exhibition narrative at the Phoenix Art Museum, 2000, and relevant sources listed in the bibliography.

2 Other than works of Kandinsky, Kazimir Malevich's oil painting the *Quadrilateral*, commonly called the *Black Square*, 1914–1915 is most easily identifiable in the West.

3 Museums of art in Czarist Russia exhibited solely representational art, and the traditional media and subjects of still life, portraits, and landscapes.

By 1919, Lenin was desperate to promote change broadly and rapidly. To activate this gargantuan cultural and political shift, he envisioned using the avant-garde as his supreme propagandizing tool. He depended heavily on these artists to provide the unspoken word of "change." In order to speak to the masses, especially those illiterate peasants in distant regions, he provided Vladimir Tatlin with funds to acquire works by contemporary artists. Naturally, the avant-garde artists welcomed this ready source of income, as well as the concept of creating museums throughout Russia and other Soviet republics where finally their work could be shown.

Between 1919 and 1922, 1211 pieces of avant-garde art and sculpture were distributed to newly constructed museums devoted entirely to modern art, the first anywhere. These museums were constructed in 36 outlying cities and distant republics as far away as Turkestan. This move provided the symbolic renouncement by the new government of the entrenched culture and art of the church and of the Czarist regime.

Avant-garde art had long been rejected by the traditional exhibitions in St. Petersburg and Moscow. Therefore they had held their own private exhibitions in large cities between 1910 and 1919. Interest in, and attendance of these exhibits had usually been confined to a small, like-minded body of well-informed elite. Therefore, the fact their work would now be on permanent display throughout the republics, was welcomed with a level of gratitude that was understandable. Through this, Lenin also had another purpose. He not only established an alliance with the art community to meet his initial goals, he sought to obligate them further. Through art, he would use them as agents of propaganda for the rigid political mandates yet to be declared.

Art schools sponsored by the government had sprung up, enabling students to explore the use of materials and expand their creative ideas. This reached its zenith by 1922. With the populace now attuned to the visual arts for their information about change, they were brain-washed to accept the message henceforth invoked by the art of Socialist Realism. Under Stalin, in addition to other propaganda, enormous billboard art masked the repeated crop failure and starvation throughout the republics.

The avant-garde stalwarts had served their purpose. They could no longer be countenanced in lieu of their progressive and even democratic expression as individuals. Despite the prominent, crucial, and dedicated role in advancing the Revolution, these forward thinkers throughout art and other cultural fields quickly became expendable. With Stalin's rise to power, many were banished to harsh oblivion, in the gulags of Siberia, the Urals, and the White Sea.

The avant-garde art which had been distributed far and wide was so appreciated by the illiterate peasants, that they preserved it at the risk of their own lives. Only after Gorbachev's loosening of restraints in 1985 and the introduction of glasnost two years later were these peasants free to divulge the secrets they had long-ago secured behind false walls.[4]

There is a further piece of irony. The Communist's suppression of religion closed the doors of the Russian Orthodox churches. However, the highly revered icons that came from the Russian Orthodox church schools of icon painting in the 12th to 15th Centuries, had embedded an imprint on the art of the avant-garde. Paradoxically, the flat, non-realistic human form embodied in the icons laid the foundation for the simplistic form and line that was characteristic of 20th century Russian abstract art.[5]

Religion had been taken from the masses. They needed something to believe. How ironic that the Revolution was to provide them abstract art with its own unintended historic and religious roots.

A few of the well-informed elite in the west and museums in Europe and the United States had small collections of this art preceding WW I. However, the broader work of the avant-garde and their contributions to the early development of abstract art have become known to the general public only recently. Thankfully, over the past decade the Russian government has released a number of these museum pieces for world tour. The public is deeply indebted to the courageous peasants who preserved these magnificent examples of the Russian avant-garde art for posterity.

---

4 Primarily canvases were preserved, since concealing sculpture presented unmanageable problems.

5 In many respects, the form of Malevich's figures circa 1928-1932 are almost iconic. The faceless figures were painted originally as a way to refute realism. Those created in the later (1928-1932) period may also signify the repression of free expression, as one way to adapt under Stalinism. Malevich himself had been an ardent member of the Russian Orthodox Church, and never abandoned his allegiance to it, albeit in secret. He died in his apartment of natural causes in 1935.

Illustrations: Titles and Captions[1]

1. *Earthquake in Egypt:* 22" × 28" pastel is done on charcoal paper, then cut; the pieces are juxtaposed and floated over the mat. 1999 (1) (See front cover.)
2. *Vermont Foliage:* 22" × 25" pastel on canvas board, adapted from a Storrs (commercial) pastel. 2001 (See page 2.)
3. *Original hand-embroidered piece:* 20" × 24" bas-relief embellishment of a floral print from India with a contoured mat. 1989 (5) (See page 6.)
4. *Viking Ship:* 16" × 18" hand-embroidered bas-relief technique (3) on cotton adapted from a piece of Danish jewelry; pastels applied with finger tip to surface and to the contour of the sculpture-cut mat. 1998 (4) (See page 8.)
5. *The* Nina, *the* Pinta, *and the* Santa Maria*:* 17" × 28" hand-embroidered to embellish printed fabric of unknown source and create abstract lines of interest, on polyester crepe. 1999 (See page 10.)
6. *Pyramids in Abstract:* 23" × 29", pastels on black mat board, cut, juxtaposed, and mounted on charcoal paper, the second in this series. 1999 (See page 14.)
7. *Dahlia:* 18" × 24" hand-embroidered to embellish a printed fabric from India attached to background fabric. 1998 (See page 16.)
8. *End of the River:* 22" × 28" first in this series of cut-apart art technique, using charcoal paper. 1999 (See page 18.)
9. *Northern Lights:* 10" × 21" hand-embroidered to embellish printed fabric of unknown source. 1998 (See page 20.)
10. *de Ruyter Reservoir:* 16" × 20" hand-embroidered original design with watercolor pencils, blended with damp paint brush on Dupioni silk. 2000 (7) (Location: de Ruyter Reservoir near Cortland, New York, named for the famous 17th century Dutch Admiral.) (See page 22.)
11. *The Adirondacks in the Abstract:* 17" × 20" hand-embroidered original design with watercolor pencils, blended with damp paint brush on Dupioni silk. 2000 (Location: Lake Champlain, Vermont.) (See page 22.)
12. *The* Mayflower*:* 17" × 21" hand-embroidered original design adapted from assorted references and drawings of ships of this era, on cotton. 1998 (See page 26.)
13. *Ships Then and Now:* 15" × 20" abstract of four ships, such as those that brought refugees and immigrants to our shores: the three-mast schooner, the frigate, the windjammer, the ocean liner at dock (yellow) using watercolor pencils on polyester, hand-embroidered in bas-relief. 1999 (See page 28.)
14. *Wooden Cross:* 14" × 17" pastel on watercolor paper of the cross and the shadows cast by it that hangs in the chancel of the Kearsarge Community Presbyterian Church, New London, New Hampshire. 2001 (See page 30.)
15. *Arched Window:* 20" × 29" watercolor on watercolor paper cut and mounted on charcoal paper, sculpture-cut mat. 1999 (See page 32.)
16. *Sail into the Sunset...Sail to the West:* 19" × 25" hand-embroidered bas-relief embellishment on printed cotton fabric from Bali. 1998 (See page 36.)
17. *Round Barn at Shelburne Farms:* 17" × 21" hand-embroidered original drawing on cotton, using watercolor pencils, with sculpture-cut mat. 1999 (Location: Shelburne, Vermont.) (See page 38.)
18. *Poppies by Design:* 17" × 21" hand-embroidered embellishment of Indian Madras plaid mounted on cotton. 1999 (2) (See page 40.)
19. *Queen Anne's Lace:* 8" × 18" hand embroidered bas-relief original design on Dupioni silk. 1999 (See page 42.)

1 Numbers in parentheses refer to techniques and are cited at the end.

20. *Stone Faces of Easter Island:* 17" × 40" original abstract design in bas-relief on polyester using watercolor pencil and blended with damp brush before doing hand embroidery. 1999 (See page 43.)

21. *White Iris:* 15" × 29" hand-embroidered bas-relief technique of original drawing of iris on polyester, tinted with watercolor pencils and blended with damp paint brush, sculpture-cut mat. 1999 (4) (#5 and #6 are a matched pair) (See page 44.)

22. *Purple Iris:* 15" × 29" hand-embroidered bas-relief technique of original drawing on two shades of polyester, tinted with watercolor pencils and blended with damp paint brush, sculpture-cut mat. 1999 (See page 45.)

23. *Ruby Anemone:* 17" × 18" hand-embroidered bas-relief original design using pastels on colored polyester and mounted within a black sculpture-cut mat over black foam core. 1998 (See page 46.)

24. *Vermont Sugar House:* 20" × 26" pastel on charcoal paper adapted from an original photograph by Clyde Smith of the Powell sugar house in Pomfret, Vermont. This photograph appeared in the Spring issue of the 1972 *Vermont Life* magazine and is included here with permission of Mr. Smith. 2000 (See page 50.)

25. *Green Mountains of Vermont:* 11" × 15" abstract design using colored mat board, in which multiple layers of each piece are cut simultaneously on the scroll saw and positioned for depth of effect by placing them from back to front; rail fence in ink. 1996 (See page 52.)

26. *Vermont History in the Abstract:* 16" × 32" hand-embroidered embellishment of fabric of unknown source, mounted on fabric mat. Symbols include: rolls of hay top and bottom; "Little Champ," Lake Champlain's beloved monster, in the upper left; the Morgan Horse, apple tree, to the left; oak tree, sumac, bayberry center left; the Vermont State bird, a goldfinch, center right; poplar trees in autumn, with bluebird on top lower left; symbol of the ship *Philadelphia* of Benedict Arnold's fleet lower right. A replica of this, as well as a ship of this fleet that was recovered from Lake Champlain, are both housed at the Maritime Museum on Basin Harbor Road, Vergennes, Vermont. 1999 (See page 54.)

27. *Blue Spruce:* 20" × 22" hand-embroidered bas-relief embellishment of printed fabric of unknown source I interpreted as blue spruce needles. 1998 (See page 58.)

28. *Peony for Diana:* 13" × 17" hand-embroidered bas-relief embellishment of printed fabric of unknown source and sculpture-cut mat. I was doing this at the time of Princess Diana's fatal accident. Many were placing flowers in front of Buckingham Palace. I felt I too had a flower for her. 2000 (See page 60.)

29. *Sailing on Lake Mascoma:* 15" × 24" pastels on tracing paper with pen and ink; hillsides, drawn as parallelograms in the style of Kazimir Malevich, foremost Russian avant-garde artist whose work I was studying at that time. 2001 (See page 62.)

30. *Vases and Bottles in the Abstract:* 17" × 20" hand-embroidered bas-relief abstract design using watercolor pencils on Dupioni silk with silk embroidery thread for much of the work. 2000 (See page 64.)

31. *Two Decanters in the Abstract:* 11" × 13" pen and ink abstract on charcoal paper. 2001 (See page 66.)

32. *My rendition of Liubov Popova's* Architectonics, 1918: 21" × 24" pastel copied from a photograph in the exhibit catalog for *Painterly Revolution: Kandinsky, Malevich and the Russian Avant-Garde*, printed here with permission. 2000 (See page 68.)

33. *Vase and Decanter:* 13" × 15" pen and ink abstract, including cut-apart art technique on charcoal paper. 2001 (See page 70.)

34. *Abstract Pitcher:* 10" × 19" self-hardening clay done in the style of Aristarhk Archipenko, artist of the Russian avant-garde, whose work I was studying at the time. 2001 (See page 70.)

35. *Bear:* 8" high, ceramic, fired clay, matt glaze, made in class at Syracuse University. 1945 (See page 72.)

36. *Landscape on the Volga:* 4" × 6" oil pastels and ink on Strathmore 400-1 sketch pad, from shipboard on the Volga between Yarlslavl and Kostroma. 2003 (See page 74.)

37. *August Skies Bode Winter's Approach:* 4" × 6" oil pastels and ink on Strathmore 400-1 sketch pad, from shipboard on the Volga. 2003 (See page 74.)

38. *Ominous Skies Open, like Glasnost:* 4" × 6" oil pastels and ink on Strathmore 400-1 sketch pad, from shipboard on the Volga. 2003 (See page 75.)

39. *Churches of the Kremlin:* 18" × 24" pastel on tracing paper shaded with tip of the finger, using a second layer beneath to add depth. 2002 (See page 76.)

40. *Cinderella's Slipper:* 16" × 15" pastel on white typing paper floated above black mat. 1995 (See page 78.)

41. *Wildflowers in the Cairngorms:* 11" × 12" pastel on canvas board adapted from photo of unknown source with wildflowers to include vast amounts of lupine of all colors, I remember seeing in 1960 on a trip through the Cairngorm Mountains of Scotland. 2001 (See page 80.)

42. *Wild Orchid:* 17" × 21" watercolor on wet watercolor paper in accord with the techniques learned under Jeanne Carbonetti of Chester, Vermont. This was transferred to Egyptian cotton for a hand-embroidered bas-relief and matted on heavy polyester fabric. 1998 (8) (See page 82.)

43. *Chrysanthemum:* 22" × 29" second in the series of cut-apart art, edges of base of vase slightly elevated so that when viewed from the right, the effect is different than when viewed from left. 2001 (See page 82.)

44. *Iris in Blue:* 5" × 16" hand-embroidered bas-relief original design that was transferred to Egyptian cotton from the first watercolor I did under the instruction of Jeanne Carbonetti. 1999 (See page 84.)

45. *Lavender Anemone:* 17" × 21" hand-embroidered bas-relief from original drawing on colored polyester using watercolor pencils blended with damp brush, sculpture-cut mat. By placing a sheet of coarse sandpaper below the cloth and rubbing it in a circular pattern, I establish the location for more than a hundred French knots in the center. Shading of the petals is done with dry pastels on the tip of the finger. 2001 (See page 84.)

46. *Tulip:* 9" × 12" original drawing of tulip on colored polyester with watercolor pencil blended with damp brush, hand-embroidered in bas-relief and mounted in a sculpture-cut mat. 1999 (See page 86.)

47. *Casablanca Lily:* 16" × 20" hand-embroidered bas-relief of the original drawing of Casablanca lily on white polyester with sculpture-cut mat and a translucent backing to hang in the window. Textured petals characteristic of this lily are created by a series of French knots. 2001 (See page 86.)

48. *Life's Mysterious Puzzle:* 22" × 29" third in this series, pastel on charcoal paper, drawn at the conclusion of writing this book of poetry. 2006 (See page 88.)

49. *Life's Many Stages and Interactions:* 18" × 23" hand-embroidered bas-relief original design on Dupioni silk using watercolor pencils, blended with damp brush; silk embroidery floss is used in some areas. 1999 (7) (See page 90.)

50. *Star of David:* 12" × 12" hand-embroidered bas-relief; design adapted from the Star of David, drawn on Egyptian cotton. 1998 (See page 95.)

51. *Bottles in the Abstract:* 16" × 20" hand-embroidered bas-relief original design on Dupioni silk using silk embroidery floss for much of the piece. 2000 (See back cover.)

---

1. Unless otherwise noted dry, not oil, pastels are used.
2. Embroidery floss is cotton, unless cited as silk.
3. Throughout my "thread and needle art" I have used a bas-relief technique. This refers to a low level of contrast, achieved here by using a thin padding between front and back cloth surfaces. The bas-relief effect occurs through the embroidery.
4. Sculpture-cut mat is created by adhering a mat board to foam core and then using a scroll saw to cut out the interior.
5. Contoured mat, same as above, with single piece of mat board and no foam core.
6. No fixative is used over watercolor pencils or pastels on fabric.
7. Imported Italian silk.
8. Jeanne Carbonetti, author of numerous books on watercolor technique. (See Bibliography, next page.)

Bibliography

Axelrod, Alan Ph.D. and Charles Philips. *What Every American Should Know About American History.* Holbrook, MA: Bob Adams, Inc., 1992.

Barron, Stephanie and Tuchman, Maurice, Editors. *The Avant-Garde in Russia 1910–1930, New Perspectives.* July 8–September 28, 1980, Los Angeles County Museum of Art, 1980.

Bayer, Henry. *The Belgians—First Settlers in New York and the Middle States.* New York: The Devin–Adair Company, 1925.

Blok, Petrus, Johannes. *History of People of the Netherlands,* vol. II. New York and London: G. P. Putnam and Sons, 1898. (Petrus Johannes Blok was Professor of History, University of Leyden at the time. Translation by Ruth Putnam.)

Blok, Petrus Johannes. *History of People of the Netherlands,* vol. IV. New York, and London: G. P. Putnam Sons, The Knickerbocker Press, 1902. (Translation by Oscar A. Bierstadt.)

Bowlt, John E. and Drutt, Matthew, Editors. *Amazons of the Avant-Garde: Exter, Goncharova, Popova, Rozonava, Stepanova and Udaltsova.* New York: Harry N. Abrams, Inc., 2000.

Brodhead, John Romeyn, Ph.D. *History of the State of New York* vol. I. New York: Harpers Bros., 1853.

Carbonetti, Jeanne. *The Tao of Watercolor, A Revolutionary Approach to the Practice of Painting.* New York: Watson-Guptil Publications, 1998.

Costobel, Eva Deutsch. *The Jews of Nieuw Amsterdam.* New York: Atheneum, 1988.

Douglas, Charlotte. *Swans of Other Worlds, Kazimir Malevich and the Origins of Abstraction in Russia.* Ann Arbor: UMI Research Press, 1976, 1980.

Griffis, William Elliot. *The Story of the Walloons, at Home, in Lands of Exile and in America.* New York: Houghton & Mifflin, 1923.

Homberger, Eric. *The Historical Atlas of New York City.* New York: Henry Holt and Company, Inc., 1994.

Hosking, Geoffrey. *Russian and the Russians, A History.* Cambridge, MA: Harvard University Press, 2001.

Jamieson, John Franklin, Ph.D., Editor. *Narratives of New Netherland, 1609–1664.* New York: Charles Scribner, 1909.

Johnson, Donald S. *Charting of the Sea of Darkness, The Four Voyages of Henry Hudson.* Camden, Maine: International Marine, 1993.

Kamen, Henry. *The Spanish Inquisition.* New Haven: Yale Press, 1998.

Knickerbocker, Barbara. *Powder Keg.* New London, New Hampshire: BKB Press, 2008.

Kootun, Yevgeny, and Kharitonova, Irina, Editors. *Avant-Garde in Russia 1920–1930.* St. Petersburg, Russia: Aurora Art Publishers, 1996.

Lamb, Martha J. *History of the City of New York: its origin, rise and progress.* New York: A. S. Barnes Company, 1877.

Lodder, Christina. *Russian Constructivism.* New Haven: Yale University Press, 1983.

Marley, David. *War of the Americas: A Chronology of Armed Conflict in the New World, 1492 to the Present.* ABC, CLIO, Santa Barbara, 1998.

Masse, Suzanne. *Land of the Firebird, The Beauty of Old Russia.* New York: Simon Schuster, 1980.

Origins of the Russian Avant-Garde. February 13–May 25, Walters Museum of Art, Baltimore, MD, 2003.

Painting Revolution: Kandinsky, Malevich and the Russian Avant-Garde. Published on the occasion of the exhibit by the same name for International Arts and Education, Baltimore, MD, the State Russian Museum and the State Museum Exhibition Center, St. Petersburg, Russia, 2000. Dates of exhibit at Phoenix Art Museum, April–July 2, 2000.

Pool, David de Sola, Ph.D. "The Mill Street Synagogue (1730–1817) of the Congregation of Shearith Israel." American Jewish Historical Society Publication, New York, New York, 1930.

Pool, David de Sola, Ph.D., and Pool, Tamar de Sola. *An Old Faith in the New World; portrait of Shearith Israel, 1654–1954.* New York: Columbia University Press, 1955.

Riker, James. *The Revised History of Harlem, its Origins and Early Annals.* New York: New Harlem Publishing Company, 1904.

Rosenfeld, Alla and Dodge, Norton T., Editors. *From Gulag to Glasnost.* New York: Thames and Hudson, Inc., 1995.

Rowell, Margit and Wye, Deborah. *The Russian Avant-Garde Book 1910–1934.* New York: The Museum of Modern Art, distributed by Harry N. Abrams, Inc., 2000.

Shearith Israel, 1654 Congregation of Shearith Israel, Spanish and Portugese Synagogue, http/www.shephardichouse.com/identity/shearithisrael.htm.

Stokes, I. N. Philip. *The Iconography of Manhattan Island 1498–1909.* New York: Robert H. Dodd, 1916.

The Vincent Family, Descendants of Adrian Vincent. Millbrook, New York: Millbrook Press, 1959. (Compiled principally by Anne M. Vincent. After her death, it was determined at the 1955 Vincent Family Reunion that Clifford Buck name a committee to complete her research. They included: Gordon S. V. Andrews, Mrs. Harrie D. Knickerbocker, and E. Harold Vincent.)

Valentine, David. *The History of the City of New York.* New York: G. P. Putnam, 1853.

Viele, Kathryn Knickerbacker. *Sketches of Allied Families: Knickerbacker–Viele Historical and Genealogical Data.* New York, Tobias A. Wright, 1916. (75 copies printed)

About the Author/Artist

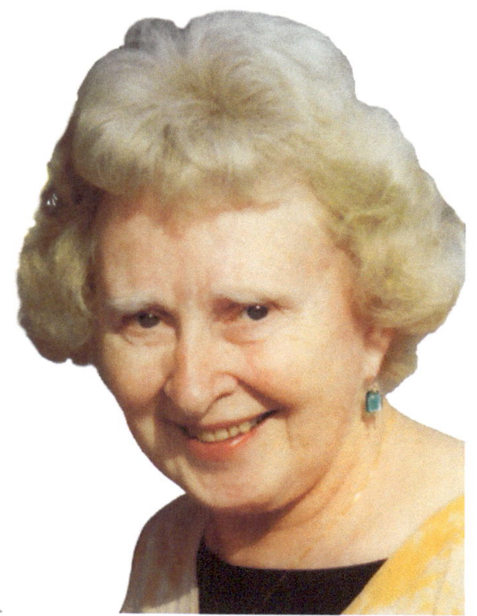

The author, aboard the *Lomonosov* on the Volga near Kostroma, 2003.

Barbara Knickerbocker (Beskind) was born in Washington, D.C., but grew up in the Hudson River Valley, at Bangall, New York, near Poughkeepsie and Hyde Park. She graduated from Green Mountain Junior College in 1943, and from Syracuse University in 1945 before going on to the Milwaukee–Downer College for Women to take her training for occupational therapy.

Her professional career spanned 46 years, the first 20 of which she was commissioned in the Army Medical Specialist Corps, serving in Army hospitals in the U.S. and overseas, as well as being Asst. Director of the Army School of Occupational Therapy at Fort Sam Houston, Texas.

After retiring as a major, she established the first free-standing private practice in occupational therapy in the United States, treating children and adults with learning disabilities. Her textbook on this subject was published in 1980 and has been used world-wide in English-speaking curricula.

Barbara, a writer of long standing began yet another career, launching the BKB Press in the spring of 2008. *Powder Keg,* the first book in a trilogy of "windows on history," was published in May, 2008. It is an historical autobiography of her life and the role of distant ancestors in history. *Touches of Life in Time and Space* is the second. She has a passionate interest in art of the Russian avant-garde (1910–1922) and this is the subject of her third "window on history," with expected date of release in 2009.

BKB Press plans to publish three titles this year, and possibly as many in 2009. BKB Press publishes mainly biography and books of historical interest.

Barbara lives in New London, New Hampshire. She moved here three years ago after living in Vermont more than 20 years, a state that is dear to her heart.

www.ingramcontent.com/pod-product-compliance
Lightning Source LLC
LaVergne TN
LVHW070132110826
845147LV00002B/235

* 9 7 8 0 9 8 1 7 7 6 8 2 8 *